THE SOD HOUSE

THE
SOD HOUSE

Cass G. Barns

UNIVERSITY OF NEBRASKA PRESS • LINCOLN

First Bison Book printing: February, 1970

Manufactured in the United States of America

Published by arrangement with Viola F. Barnes

CONTENTS

Page

Foreword—Hon. Addison E. Sheldon.. 3

Preface—By Author 7

Chapter I—Westward Emigration 11

Chapter II—Birth of Nebraska.. 19

Chapter III—More or Less Personal....................................... 31

Chapter IV—Ways of the Country... 45

Chapter V—A Sod House Home... 57

Chapter VI—Indians—Buffalo—Game 72

Chapter VII—Grasshoppers—Drouth—Colonization 89

Chapter VIII—The Nebraska Climate....................................106

Chapter IX—Pioneer Country Schools..................................115

Chapter X—Railroad Land Grants—Taxes—Free Passes.....125

Chapter XI—Live Stock and Grain Dealers..........................135

Chapter XII—District Court During the Eighties...................146

Chapter XIII—Nebraska Politics 156

Chapter XIV—Character Sketches 179

Chapter XV—Ox Team Freighting.......................................197

Chapter XVI—A Pioneer Preacher.......................................208

Chapter XVII—The Weekly Newspaper—Pioneer Poets........219

Chapter XVIII—The Money Loaner 233

Chapter XIX—The Sod House Doctor...................................244

Chapter XX—Grand Army of the Republic...........................253

Chapter XXI—Evolution of Nebraska National Guard...........263

Chapter XXII—Nebraska National Guard in Action...............272

FOREWORD

The history of Plymouth Colony was written by
William Bradford, the second governor of the
colony, who came over on the Mayflower in 1620,
became governor in 1621 and wrote his history in
the years 1630-1650. This manuscript history of
the first successful English Colony in the northern
states, in some unaccountable way, was carried to
England before the Revolutionary War. For two
hundred years it was given up as lost. It was discovered in 1855 in an English library and was
printed by the Massachusetts Historical Society in
1856.

The history of Plymouth Colony, as we now know
it from the intimate, personal narrative of Governor William Bradford, never would have been
known to the world if this manuscript had not been
discovered. Other members of the Plymouth
Colony lived their lives in the foundation period of
that famous settlement and their knowledge died
with them. A few fragments of the story of the
colony in the form of personal letters and brief
sketches survived. But the true history of the
colony, written by the man best equipped for telling
its story and giving an inside view of what the men
and women of Plymouth Colony thought and said,
as well as what they did, comes down to us through
this William Bradford manuscript which was lost
for two hundred years.

The intimate story of Nebraska in the period of
its white settlement can only be known through the

personal narratives of the men and women who were part of those settlements, who lived the life themselves, who knew the daily thoughts and daily events of the community. And most of all by those who were equipped by literary training, by personal sympathy and by the gift of imagination which made it possible for them to see the real significance of events about them in the years of the founding of Nebraska.

For such a work, Doctor Cass G. Barns, of Madison, is most fortunately equipped to write the intimate story of the settlement and the frontier years of that part of central Nebraska lying between the Elkhorn and Loup rivers and including the counties of Nance, Boone, Antelope, and Madison. Dr. Barns at the outset was a country doctor, who combined farming with medicine. Later he had part in the founding and management of the first industries of Boone county. Later he became the editor of a country newspaper, county commissioner, and still later postmaster, and again editor. All his life Dr. Barns has been in politics, taking an active part in the movements of public thought and affairs. All his life Dr. Barns has lived in sympathetic relation with the people of his region, with a natural wit for interpreting life, and with a memory able to store away the significant events within the range of his observations.

Now in his mature later years, Dr. Barns has undertaken to tell the story of the foundations of Nebraska in that rich and picturesque prairie land where his life has been spent. No one in all that region is so well equipped for this task. No one so well knows the life of pioneer settlements as the country doctor, and the country editor, and it might be added, the country postmaster who (in the popular pioneer belief) knew every letter written or received by every person in the community and read all the postal cards.

As Superintendent of the Nebraska State Historical Society, I am rejoiced to extend welcome to this history written by Dr. Barns. It preserves for all future generations a faithful picture of the period and the region which it describes. I am glad to recommend it to the pioneers, to their descendants, and to the uncounted multitudes who shall dwell in Nebraska through the ages. I have some special knowledge of this field from my own service as the editor of a country newspaper in Madison County during these pioneer years. I am rejoiced that Dr. Barns' experiences are not dying with him and that they will not be lost through the centuries as Governor William Bradford's history of the Plymouth Colony was lost.

ADDISON E. SHELDON,

Superintendent and Secretary,
Nebraska State Historical Society.

August 25, 1930.

PREFACE

These reminiscent, historical and biographical sketches reciting the activities of the pioneer home-makers of the first thirty years of Nebraska statehood, are not offered as fiction, because I know from personal observation, or from having received them from reliable sources, that most of them are true. Neither is it claimed that as assembled they are entitled to a place in literature.

Rather they are presented as the activities of a virile, red-blooded, industrious plain people who followed the territorial pioneers and accomplished the actual development of the prairies. They built upon the foundation laid by those hardy men who drove the wild men and wild animals from the fertile land, and prepared it for prosperous homes, schools, churches, transportation systems, that brought city and farm wealth. They changed a land used as battle fields of warring savages into a land of peace, prosperity, plenty and obedience to law. They turned the pastures of wild buffalo, deer and antelope into a land that protected and developed a high class of improved farm animals. Where the Indian, the outlaw, the horse thief, the gunman, the murderer, the dance hall and gambling hell depraved denizen ruled, only restrained by lynch law administered by regulators, the builders of Nebraska changed it all into a land of prosperous and refined homes and orderly procedure of law. Growing crops, fine farm homes, fine towns and a happy people replaced a land in the state of nature.

Those wonderful people are fast being gathered to their final homes and it is my effort to present and perpetuate a class of people, rather than individuals while there is yet time before the opportunity is forever lost. It is to make it possible for the successors of the pioneers to see with the eyes of the pioneers of the sod house period, and follow the labors, hardships, disappointments, successes, sickness and deaths of the builders of this great state as well as to record their successes and joys.

Men and women in the strength of early manhood and early womanhood came from all parts of the United States and even from overseas. They brought with them the traditions and customs of the people with whom they had lived. They would have been gratified had they been able to build upon the foundation of the land and people they had grown up among. In the new country they met hundreds of others who came from every section of the country, who also brought customs and traditions of the people with whom they had associated. All these were thrown into the common melting pot, to mix and finally develop a product that was not representative of any one former home or people but a union of them all.

The strong and able men and women of the older states saw the door of opportunity opening to them. The latch string was outside the door and a welcome to come in met those who were knocking for admittance. Many came who failed to secure the success they hoped to attain. Many suffered casualties or returned to their former homes and friends but many poor boys attained distinction and secured property and homes beyond their most sanguine expectation. It has been estimated that an average of two and a half settlers filed on free government land for every one that remained and secured a home.

On an Illinois rented farm a large family became so crowded that the oldest son found a lack of room in the home nest. He was strong and brave and 18 years old. He left home with $15.00 in his pocket and only the clothes on his back and walked to the territory of Nebraska. When he reached the land of his hopes he was penniless and barefoot. By industry and taking advantage of opportunities he assembled a goodly amount of property. He was honored by his neighbors by elevation to the state legislature and later was elected to several terms in the United States Congress.

Another poor boy became an attorney at law and held several positions of trust and was finally elected judge of the supreme court of the state. What it meant to him was well told in his own words written to a friend: "Perhaps no poorer boy ever came to Nebraska than I. And yet because big brave men have stood by me, I find myself in what seems to me the most exalted position in the state. The most that I can claim for myself is this: no matter what position I was in or what I was given to do, I have done my best. I have entered upon my new duties determined to pursue this course and trust that my work may vindicate the judgment of my friends."

What better explanation of the door of opportunity opening to those who knock could be given? The spirit of the Nebraska pioneer and homesteader is shown in the success of those two young men whose experience was shared by hundreds of others. Not only the spirit, but the composite product of the Nebraska melting pot is shown in the statement made by the judge.

By preserving the activities, incentives and ambitions of a plain and possibly crude people, in a plain crude way, before it is overlooked for more pretentious matters, is the aim of this volume. The territorial settlers chose and cleared the ground but it was the homesteaders of the sod house period between 1867 and 1897 who shaped the course and held the helm of the Nebraska ship of state and steered it into the safe harbor of completed statehood.

CASS G. BARNS.

CHAPTER I

Westward Emigration

"Adieu, adieu, my native shore
Fades o'er the water blue;
The night winds sigh, the breakers roar,
And shrieks the wild sea mew.
Yon sun that sets upon the sea,
We follow in his flight;
Farewell awhile to him and thee,
My native land—Good-night."
—*Byron.*

HE natural tide of emigration of the human race trends westward. Great bodies of restless people invaded Europe from the east during historic times. Tradition brings my ancestors across the English channel to barbarous England, and that William the Conqueror rewarded him for prowess in conflict by the gift of a goodly heritage of wooded land in central England. Be it as it may, one of his descendants, who was filled with wanderlust, and optimism about the newly discovered country across the ocean, embarked for the New England shores hoping to possess some of the goodly land.

About the year 1632 Thomas Barns embarked on a small sailing vessel that was leaving England, bound for the pioneer shores of what was later called New England. Landing on the bleak, rocky shore, he sought to establish himself in a new colony. Authorities differ somewhat as.to the year of his arrival. It may have been earlier than 1632 and some affirm that he came over in a late voyage of the Mayflower. Anyway, he soon made the para-

mount feature of the American settler apparent by
listening to stories of the wonderful opportunities
to the westward. Reports told of the fertile Connecticut valley with its fine pasture and hay land
and rich bottom land, all waiting the adventurous
settler. All that was required was to dispossess
the people occupying it as Caleb did the occupants
of the heritage given him in the Promised Land.
Records show that he went to the Connecticut valley
with one of the first parties and was soon engaged
in the war with the Indians.

At this time the first great clash between organized whites and tribal Indians occurred. Naturally
the Indians resented the encroachment of the white
people who were occupying their best land and killing the game that gave them a part of their food.
They were, also, cultivating much land that they
cropped to corn, beans, pumpkins, etc. This in some
instances the white settlers were possessing.

Depredations by the Indians brought reprisals
by the settlers. An Indian war that lasted for some
time resulted in the defeat of the Indians and the
destruction of their forts, villages and huts. The
most decisive battle was a surprise on an Indian
palisaded fort or village on a hill called Mistick,
and later Pequot Hill. It is the present site of the
village of Groton, Connecticut. The barking of a
dog gave the first warning to the Indians, who were
asleep. The attacking white settlers were members
of several militia companies under command of experienced Indian fighters. They burned the fort and
slew most of the Indians inside the palisades, or
killed them while they were trying to escape. Several of the attacking force were killed or seriously

wounded, and they estimated that seven hundred
Indians were killed, but as the attacking party did
not remain to count them, the actual Indian loss
was conjecture. It was a frightful defeat for the
Indians and as a result of their losses and the somewhat drawn-out campaign the Indians became disheartened and accepted their defeat and many of
them emigrated. Thomas Barns served during the
campaign and at the reduction of the Pequot fort.

The Mohican tribe admitted a loss of four hundred and the survivors emigrated to the far west.
They have been called the lost tribe of Mohicans
and their new location became a matter of doubt.
We hear of them again in northern Indiana, many
years later, where they were alleged to have settled.

As a reward for services during the Indian wars,
Thomas Barns was given six acres of land
within the present city of Hartford, Connecticut,
and a portion of it remained in possession of his
descendants for many years. He was also given
fifty acres of farming land in the adjacent
country.

Agreeable to the benign religious administration
of the early New Englanders, Thomas Barns' first
wife was executed for witchcraft. His second wife
was mother of my ancestor. Later, members of the
Barns family settled in western Massachusetts and
participated in the war of the revolution. The next
family trek was to Kings county, New York state.
Then a soldiers' warrant was laid upon a tract of
land in Onondaga county, New York. The occupants of that land experienced all the privations,
hardships and joys of back woods settlers. History
gives them a place in the making of a new civiliza-

tion as the progress of the white man kept its westward course.

The country was growing old and crowded when
my father loaded his family, consisting of wife and
five children, into a prairie schooner and started
on a pilgrimage to northern Indiana, where a few
acquaintances had preceded him. There was land
and to spare and he hoped to carve out a new home
in the big forests, as his forbears had in New York
state.

Following the Erie canal westward to Lake Erie
they embarked on a steamer for Toledo. At Toledo
they saw their first railroad. Strap iron was fastened to logs laid lengthwise over which a small
steam engine drew loads. Taking a westward
course after a long journey over the frightful pioneer roads, through the woods and swamps, and
fording streams, he arrived at his destination west
of South Bend and Mishawauka, Indiana, in the
Potawattamie Indian country, at the southern end
of Lake Michigan. There father, travel weary,
finding a tract of land that resembled York State,
with sugar maple trees, spring brook and gravelly
loamy soil, announced that his moving days were
over. It was some years later that I appeared and
established family relationship with the other brothers and sisters and became a Hoosier pioneer.

My early days were spent working on father's
farm and teaching country schools. In time I aspired to become a country doctor. After the necessary preparation I made ready for people to trust
their lives in my hands. I did not solicit patients,
or take orders, but waited their call. I found great
opportunity to do good and filled the cemeteries in

A Northern Indiana Sugar Maple Grove.

An Indiana settler's log cabin. It is an excellent illustration of a pioneer's home in the woods during the winter season. The pioneer family doctor is seen approaching the cabin to make a professional call. The snow drifts have compelled him to make his rounds on horseback.

proportion to my opportunities. Opportunities were great to serve mankind by a quiet removal of world weary or objectionable citizens but I always let nature take its course with the survivors of the nasty tasting medicine of the time. It was a snowy country and the northwest winds off Lake Michigan were, to say the least, invigorating when the temperature ranged twenty below. Drifts frequently covered eight rail stake and ridered rail fence so that detours were made over the top into fields where snow laid thinner. The horse and cutter negotiated those snow road detours readily.

The countless small swamps in the timber land and decaying vegetation on the prairie when the breaking plow had done its work, made ideal breeding places for mosquitos. It was not known at the time that mosquitos were malaria carriers, and little effort was made to guard against them by protecting windows and doors with cloth netting. Wire screen had not yet come into its own. Smudge fires to drive them away by smoke, and early bedtime, somewhat reduced the menace. An unbalanced ration of fat pork, too much fruit and exposure to the heat of August days, caused indigestion that went hand in hand with the malaria carrying mosquito, brought intermittent fevers, cholera morbus among adults, and cholera infantum among children, and filled the cabins and even the homes of prosperous people with sickness. Added to this, the typhoid carrying house fly got in his deadly work without being suspected. So the Autumn season was one ordinarily devoted to the worship of the God of Medicine. A purely malarial attack would begin with a feeling of chilliness soon after sunrise,

and an inclination to get close to a fire or sit in the
sunshine. Soon the chilliness became marked and
shaking and shivering came on that was only
checked by the coming of a hot fever. After several hours the fever was followed by perspiration
and temporary recovery. This routine might return in 72, 48 or 24 hours, or if complicated, would
become continuous with little intermission. The
period when fever was absent, or at lowest ebb, and
the skin moist, was devoted to the taking of quinine.

Sometimes the malarial attack was so severe that
the patient never rallied from the chill, and de-
pression continued till death intervened. This state
was known to Hoosiers as a congestive chill. It
took active treatment and heroic measures to bring
back the warmth of life and prepare the patient for
the life saving quinine. I recall a typical case with
all conditions present to make a congestive chill result fatally. The log cabin in the woods, the swamp
with its breeding places for mosquitos, the unsanitary environments, and a shiftless and ignorant family. The man had hook-worm symptoms and an ap-
petite for whiskey that he sought to appease whenever he could. He also had an aversion to quinine
and its bitter taste. Quinine had also been charged
with going to the bones when the neuralgia twinges
of chronic ague were felt.

I was called to a cabin in the woods to see the
head of a family who was a man noted for his pro-
fuse vocabulary and opposition to work. I found
him suffering from a congestive malarial attack, and
by vigorous work restored his circulation and left
him sufficient quinine, if taken as directed, to ward
off or lighten the expected attack next day. About

noon next day as I was starting on my rounds in an opposite direction from the sick man's cabin, I was hailed by a ragged boy running at top speed and crying in alarm for me to see his "Pap" immediately. I asked why he was alarmed and he answered that Pap was going to die. Inquiring for further information as to what his Pap was doing, he said, "He is 'ent doin' nothin'. He is setten up against the side of the house with his britches off and we can't wake him up." I realized the condition and changed my routing, not in the best of humor because I thought my instructions had not been obeyed. I found the lank, pallid Hoosier much as the boy had reported. He was unconscious, skin relaxed and oozing with cold perspiration, jaw dropped, cheeks flapping in and out, intermitting respiration, a throat gurgle and in fact he was about gone. I got his feet into hot water well fortified with mustard, rubbed his extremities vigorously, administered artificial respiration and poured a spoonful of raw whiskey into his throat and worked it down by hand. After a bit, circulation and warmth began to return and I left him with the family to continue efforts till I could visit other patients. I returned to find "Pap" had been restored to consciousness. Then Mr. Low Brow Hoosier was in for a tongue lashing. I said, "Look here, old fellow, if you want to die, go to it; it is your own business. Here was your chance. I have given you the advice and left you the medicine, that had you taken, would have brought recovery. The devil wants your company; he is reaching for you," and I made the demonstration with fingers extended, clawing for him. "He nearly got you yesterday.

He will get you tomorrow. If you want to go to him, do as you have done and save that quinine. I am through with you if you disobey my orders again."

But he was equal to the occasion and defended himself valiantly by saying that his family had practiced deception on him. They had told him that I offered him whiskey and he refused to take it, and he knew that such an unjust slander on him was a dam lie. However, he was impressed and the quinine did its work.

But Indiana pioneer days began to wane. The star of empire was drifting westward. Crowds of tramps asking for food and work, but never working, were heading toward Chicago. Hundreds of prairie schooners passed westward daily, carrying men, women and children to open a new pioneer farming country on the great plains. Indiana was becoming industrialized. The young men were leaving the farms and emigrating westward to secure farms or were going to town to work in the shops, where their morale was speedily lowered from the high standard of their resolute ancestors who were tillers of the soil. German immigrants had been doing a great part in making Indiana prosperous. Other national ties came in. Indiana ceased to occupy a place as a pioneer farming state. It became an old state as the star of empire was moving westward.

CHAPTER II

The Birth of Nebraska

"Master of human destinies am I,
 Fame, love, and fortune on my footsteps wait,
Cities and fields I walk; I penetrate
 Deserts and seas remote, and passing by
Hovel, and mart, and palace, soon or late
 I knock unbidden, once at every gate.
  I am opportunity."

—*Ingalls.*

THE United States of America made the greatest real estate purchase of valuable farming acreage the world ever knew when President Jefferson purchased the Louisiana territory from France in 1803. More remarkable, in a world given to conquest by force of arms, it was secured by treaty and peaceful negotiations. Twelve populous states, of which Nebraska was one, besides Oklahoma and some Indian reservations, have been carved from that vast tract of territory. New Orleans, the Louisiana metropolis, was first occupied by the French in 1718 and became the foremost city and capital of the territory during subsequent occupancy.

President Thomas Jefferson was assisted in his great purchase by a number of able associates but had the opposition of others. Success was made possible by the European wars. The great European wars were imminent and France and England were sparring for position. New Orleans people claim that their city has been under eight different governments. Spain had possessed the territory and with France, left her record in the mixed French and Spanish citizenship that remains to this day. Napoleon Bonaparte was wise enough to realize that in the midst of a general European war, that it would be difficult if not impossible to keep England from taking the Louisiana cession from France. Negotiations resulted in France ceding practically all of the great Mississippi valley and tributary lands to the United States for the insignificant sum of $15,000,000. France owed American citizens for various claims $3,750,000. These claims the Jefferson government agreed to assume. Bonds to the amount of $11,250,000 in full payment for nearly 900,000 square miles of fertile land, were issued and delivered to France.

Many reasons have been advanced to explain why Napoleon made such a poor sale and did it against the judgment of his advisers. The most plausible reason was that Napoleon was wiser than his statesmen. There had been minor differences between France and the United States but above it all Napoleon knew that the intervention of France in favor of the colonies during the war for independence had left a profound respect in the hearts of the common people of the young republic for France. They did not possess that respect for England and in event of general European hostilities, France stood to lose Louisiana to England. Napoleon chose to further strengthen his position by cementing friendship with the United States, rather than incur their enmity by permitting such an undesirable neighbor as England to be in a position to attack them from the rear. Without the Louisiana purchase, the United States could never have attained world domination as it has. Our national independ-

ence might have been threatened by the occupancy
of the Mississippi valley by a foreign government
leaving us a fringe of rocky territory along the
Atlantic coast between the sea and the fertile inland
country secured by the Louisiana purchase. Was
Napoleon but a link in the chain with which Providence bound our republic to civilization?

The mixed Louisiana population of Spanish,
French, Creole, and people from the West Indies
were not pleased at the transfer to the United
States. Napoleon gave them the following message
after he had made the sale and transfer of the
Louisiana territory:

"Let the Louisanians know that we separate ourselves from them with regret; that we stipulate for
everything they can desire; and let them hereafter,
happy in their new independence, recollect that they
have been Frenchmen, and that France, in ceding
them, has secured for them advantages which no
European power, however paternal, could have af-
forded. Let them retain their love for us; and may
our common origin, language and customs, perpetuate that love."

The words of Napoleon were prophetic. In less
than twelve years 8,000 picked English soldiers
tried to take the territory from the Americans as
they surely would have from the French, were defeated by American frontiersmen with frightful
slaughter on the Chalmette farm just below New
Orleans. There are descendents of the early French
now living in New Orleans who can speak little but
the French language and people fifty years of age
live within a block of the place where they were
born and are strangers to outside the city limits.

Piece by piece territorial and state allotments were carved from the great Louisiana purchase. They were always accompanied by contentions among the strong, red blooded settlers. Slavery was the leading contention and the advocates of negro slavery in the south, met midway with the free territory advocates of the north. There were clashes and border warfare but it did not extend north of the Platte river in Nebraska. Early maps show Nebraska territory comprising the present state of Nebraska, the Dakotas, Montana and some adjoining unorganized sections. Considering climate, rainfall, soil and freedom from hot winds and cyclones, no state was dealt with more generously by nature than Nebraska, yet it was called the "Great American Desert" by first explorers. Even as late as the nineties the common opinion was that farming could only be successful within 100 miles of the Missouri river. West of Kearney was considered fit for cattle grazing only. Later the unsurpassed grain section extending into Colorado, as well as the sandhill districts, are recognized as being wonderfully valuable.

The South Platte section and 100 miles on the eastern end of the North Platte district is rich loess identical with the mud in the Missouri river water. To the northwest is the sandhill country, pronounced by geologists as being the bed of an ancient lake that was gradually drained by elevation of the land. There is still a vast underflow of water in the sandhills section and where the loess deposits were pierced by the early settlers for wells, numerous submerged logs and bones of extinct animals were laid bare by the spade of the well digger. The sandhill section, formerly considered worthless except for grazing purposes, readily sustains tree life and many tracts are susceptible for grain and vegetable farming.

It is not my purpose to review the geological history of Nebraska or the Louisiana purchase, neither take up the early territorial history of Nebraska that has been so ably preserved by J. Sterling Morton and his associates. There were giants at the birth of Nebraska, young, brainy, fearless men and women. They laid out the work. I would like to perpetuate the activities of those who followed and did the detail work of developing what the fathers had prepared for them to do. The mighty army of farmers who occupied the land, enticed capital, the professions, the churches and the great transportation systems to follow and reap their share of the great reward that was realized from the hardships suffered by those who made their first homes in "dug outs" and sod houses and subdued the prolific prairie land and converted it to the use of mankind.

The Mormons established a route through Nebraska following what had been mere trails. On being driven from Illinois as undesirable citizens they started westward to find a place where they could live undisturbed. They were a narrow, uneducated, religious people who looked lightly on human life. Not all favored polygamy. They had giant intellects among them who led them and directed their movements. A stop was made at Council Bluffs in Iowa and Florence in Nebraska near Omaha and at the present site of Genoa in Nance county. Finally their advance expedition

reached the desert by the Great Salt Lake where
they established Salt Lake City. Irrigation brought
wonderful results and they were located to profit
by the travel during the gold rush to California.
The trail they had followed became the great wagon
road to the Pacific coast and by diversions, to the
Oregon district.

In 1868 when settlers began to occupy isolated
spots along the Mormon trail on the north side of
the Platte river, a colony of Polish people took up
their residence just west of the Loup river where
it empties into the Platte. Among them came
Walenty (Valentine) Jarecki and his young wife
who had been married in Prussia two years before.
Mrs. Jarecki graphically described their experiences
in establishing a new home:

"We were told in Germany that in America one
could grow rich quickly because there one could obtain land gratis. My husband and myself, being
both young and strong, we resolved to try our luck.
Upon our arrival at New York we were directed to
Nebraska. After our safe arrival at Columbus, we
were led into a sand desert, about six miles from
Columbus. 'The Lord help us,' I cried out to my
husband at the sight. Our land having been staked
off, we two remained alone under the open vault of
heaven. Our first care was to prepare a sleeping
place. We dug a hole and covered it with brushes.
Next we put up three poles and attached our pot
to it, to prepare our meals. Soon after we commenced to put up a sod house; it was without windows. Thereupon we commenced to cultivate our
land, my husband with the spade and I with the hoe.
In spring we purchased a yoke of oxen and a plow

and sowed the grain. Thus the first year ended.
Later on we obtained more land. Meanwhile Mr.
V. Lassek had arrived, our first neighbor. Whenever we wished to sell anything my husband with
an ox team left for Omaha on Monday morning and
returned on Saturday evening. In the meantime I
remained alone with the children. Frequently the
Indians paid us a visit."

The wagon roads through Illinois, Iowa and Nebraska became great national thoroughfares following the gold rush to California in 1848 and to Pikes
Peak in 1859 and again after the Civil war.

Many herds of cattle were driven from the states
to points in the mountains and even to California.
Wagon trains and cattle herds were seldom out of
sight of each other and always flanked by hostile
Indians. Not all travelers going through Nebraska
thought it was a desert and many returned to the
"states" after the Pikes' Peak gold rush with high
praise for the good farming lands on "The Plains."

A returned Californian told me his experience in
helping drive a herd of cattle to California during
the early fifties. He was a young single man living
in central northern Indiana, and a chronic sufferer
from malaria. A herd of cattle was being gathered
to drive to California and physicians advised that
he join the company of drovers, presuming that the
outdoor life would be beneficial to his health. There
were no baby beeves at that time and any animal
from a 15 year old ox to a grandmother cow was
considered "beef." The promoters of the trek gathered a large herd of this class of cattle and added
to the herd by purchase as they proceeded. The
drive lasted six months and by the time Nebraska

was reached the outdoor life had restored my informant's health.   It also found him promoted to
be herd boss.

It was his job to look ahead for places to stop at
nights and places for the cattle to pasture.   Illinois
and Iowa being new it was not so hard, yet only a
few miles a day could be traveled.   As a rule the
streams had to be forded but just before reaching
Nebraska a bridge was found across a small river.
Having passed this bridge he was with the van of
the herd when a herder who had been left to bring
up the rear came to him and told him that two Indians had an ox held up for toll for crossing the
bridge.   Inspecting the herd he noted the absence
of an ox with a crumpled horn that had been bought
near Kosciuska, Indiana.   Arriving at the bridge
he found the two Indians holding back the ox and
two of his men afraid to try to secure possession
of their property.   He ordered his men to drive the
ox across and ride over the red devils if they got
in the way.   Thereupon one Indian fired at him but
missed and he shot the Indian dead.   The other Indian ran away.   The ox joined the herd.

The same process was repeated at Wood River
in Nebraska.   Indians held the herd at a ford crossing and in the effort to retrieve the property he had
to kill another Indian.   But Nebraska had fine pasturage to get the cattle in shape for the trip through
the mountain passes and poorer pasturage to the
westward.   All through the Indian country a constant guard had to be kept, night and day, over the
cattle to save them from being stolen by Indians.

A story of the naming of Rawhide creek just east
of Fremont, Nebraska, has been told hundreds of

times with slight variations ever since the days of the California gold rush. The main part of the stories agree but the actual eye witnesses have never been located though they are just one informant away. This man who went with the herd to California told me the story of the naming of Rawhide creek as he had it from an uncle who was with the train to which the victim belonged and was present at his death. A young man, who was a member of the train, had boasted all along the way that he would shoot the first Indian he saw. He was not taken seriously, but near a small stream between the Elkhorn river and the present site of Fremont, an Indian woman was seen sitting on a log near a small stream. The young man made good his boast by shooting this woman.

Between Fremont and Ashland, on the south side of the Platte river, was a large Indian village and many small bands were scattered over the country at the time. They were at peace with the whites but they invoked their tribal laws and demanded the white man's life for the life of the murdered woman. Being surrounded by an overwhelming body of Indians, the train could do nothing but obey the demand and give up the murderer. The story always goes that the Indians stripped him and strung him up by the hands and skinned him while alive. Of course he soon died in great agony. The creek was named "Rawhide" from this example of Indian justice and remains so named to this day. It is a remarkable story and the skinning is believed to have been done. Still, from all the stories and traditions, none come closer to being proven by eye witnesses than the one my informant told who said his uncle was a member of the train and witnessed the skinning.

Possibly the story of the naming of Rawhide creek, with the frightful story of skinning a man alive, was circulated to prevent overt acts by the thoughtless people who were passing through land occupied by many Indians. There seems to be no actual proof that the story is true although many reputed eye witnesses were only one degree removed from those who told the story.

The Platte valley, following the Mormon trail along the north side of the Platte river, is a level plain about ten miles wide and about fifty miles long from the Elkhorn river on the east to the Loup river on the west. The Loup is a considerable river that empties into the Platte river at Columbus, about 90 miles west of Omaha. Many streams flow into the Loup from the north side. The first of considerable size is Beaver creek that joins the Loup about twenty miles above its confluence with the Platte river. Here was found very choice prairie land and a great body of timber in the Loup valley extending for many miles to the northwest. The State Historical Society has proven, by examination of the remains of huts, that the land had been occupied for ages. Pieces of armor taken from a lost Spanish expedition, a record of which is recorded dimly in the past, have been found by digging in ancient lodge pits. At this junction of the Beaver and Loup a detachment of Mormons were instructed to make a stopping post for the multitudes to follow on the march to Utah. They built sod houses and cultivated the rich bottom land, made ditches and sod walls to impound their cattle. They

became quite comfortable and prosperous but the
United States government allotted what is now
Nance county to the Pawnee Indians for a reservation and established the agency post near the Mormon settlement at what is now Genoa. It was admirably suited for Indian occupancy, even to the
improvements and sod houses the Mormons had
made. There was a large body of timber, choice
bottom land ideal for garden and corn and all the
lazy Indians had to do to enjoy it was to drive out
the Mormon occupants, which they did with
pleasure.

The evicted Mormons went a few miles farther
down the Loup river and again made homes and
cultivated the land. This settlement was called
Keats-ka-toos by the Indians. Many of this body
of Mormons remained in Nebraska and their descendants are still living in Columbus.

It was a paradise for the Indians, good corn
land, good pasturage, plenty of wood, streams teem-
ing with fish and water fowl. They added to the
Mormon village of sod houses by their own sod huts
covered with timber and long grass and dirt. From
this favored location they would go out annually on
a big buffalo hunt to the western part of the state.
They had to be constantly on guard against their
hereditary enemies, the Sioux Indians, but all went
along happily for some time. The government was
trying to teach them to become farmers and had
employed a man named John Williamson to show
them how to cultivate the soil. Mr. Williamson had
come from Massachusetts with a small colony that
settled in Boone county about 25 miles to the northwest.

One year the tribe went on its annual buffalo hunt to the Republican river country, leaving the old and incapacitated people at the reservation. John Williamson accompanied them. After a successful hunting season the tribe was ambushed by the Sioux and many of them were massacred. This so disheartened the tribe that they consented to be removed to the Indian Territory. The removal was successfully accomplished in 1877 and the government property at the agency was made the nucleus for a very successful Indian Industrial School where hundreds of Indian children are educated.

The large tract of timber was a Godsend to the poor settlers who came from a hundred miles away to get wood and poles for making sod houses and stock shelter. Permission was not asked or given to take the timber. It was simply winked at by government officials. Indians usually chose a high point of a hill extending from the uplands out into the valley for burying their dead. When I first saw their burying ground white people had been digging into the graves, mostly from curiosity, as the Indian's valuables were buried with him. Sometimes the government sought evidence of treaties or other agreements in the graves of the Indian chiefs.

CHAPTER III

More or Less Personal

"O wad some Pow'r the giftie gie us
To see oursels as others see us;
It wad frae monie a blunder free us
And foolish notion."
—*Burns.*

N 1878 I was a young doctor who had crowded in among fifteen or twenty older medics into the beautiful county seat town of Laporte, Indiana. I was succeeding satisfactorily in establishing myself. I had noted with great interest the passage of so called "prairie schooners" westward bound. Sometimes hundreds would pass my office in a single day. Those prairie schooners were simply farm wagons fitted with several substantial wooden bows covered with heavy muslin, and drawn by a pair of horses. The occupants were usually young families, husband, wife and two or three children. They traveled during the day and camped by the wayside at night. Their objective was Kansas or Nebraska where they hoped to establish themselves in homes of their own instead of renting farms in the older states owned by landlords.

Many wagons had mottoes or bluffy statements painted roughly on the white wagon covers. "Kansas or Bust" was seen frequently and Greeley's advice, "Go west, young man" a close second. I was interested in another, but smaller procession of covered wagons, that met the westward bound pro-

cession. They also had used the paint bush. Some
of them had added to the "Kansas or Bust," the
simple word "Busted." Others would have "Going
back to my wife's relation," printed on the wagon
cover.

Then Nebraska railroads began to advertise liberally for settlers and offer wonderful inducements
to buy their lands and settle on them. The appeal
for homesteaders to file on government land came
from immigration agents in many new county seat
towns in the new west. Great effort was made to
entice "settlers." Among the propositions was the
Pawnee reservation land in Nebraska that had just
been surveyed and offered for sale at very low
prices, one-third cash and balance on liberal terms.
Another, that looked best to me, was the efforts of
Adam Smith to dispose of the Burlington & Missouri
lands in Boone county.

During November, 1878, after a somewhat strenuous period of attending the sick, I felt justified in
taking a vacation and determined to see Nebraska
for myself, and if the land looked good, to secure
some of it while it was cheap. I had laid aside a
little nest egg but it was entirely insufficient to buy
the fine Laporte county prairie land. Accompanied
by two young men who had just passed their 21st
year, we started for Nebraska, our objective being
to examine the Pawnee Indian lands, a plat of which
I had secured from the land office at Grand Island.
I also had a circular from Adam Smith and a pam-
phlet sent out by the B. & M. railroad land department extolling the merits of their Nebraska and
Boone county holdings.

We reached Silver Creek, a station west of Columbus, about sundown and stayed there till next morning. Everything was novel and new to us. Harvey Maricle, a prominent Boone county homesteader, had just come in with a wagon load of wheat to market. Instead of bringing it in sacks, as the Hoosiers did, it was loose in an open wagon box. The grain elevator had closed for the day and he left his wheat standing unguarded in the street all night. Such a risk would not have been taken in any Indiana town.

Next morning we hired a livery team and driver to take us to inspect the Pawnee reservation lands. Going a long distance across the prairie not a single habitation was seen. The surveyors had marked the section corners and quarter section outside corners but had not subdivided the sections and established the centers. A lasting corner was made by digging sods to make a hole in each of the four directions and making a sod mound with the sods exactly where the corner should be. Those mounds lasted for years, but the cottonwood stakes the surveyors planted, indicating the description of the land were soon lost to travelers taking them to make camp fires of, or were burned when the grass burned during a prairie fire. Not finding anyone to tell us about the land and our native driver becoming lost, I directed him to drive to the Pawnee Indian agency buildings where we arrived at noon, determined to remain clear of Indian lands and see Adam Smith, whose headquarters were about fifteen miles northwest in Boone county near where the town of St. Edward was later located

An elderly man named Kilbourn was one of the
carriers of the daily mail from Columbus to Albion,
a distance of about fifty miles, and also carried pas-
sengers. He was ready to leave for Albion but
waited till we ate dinner. His bus was an open two-
seated buggy drawn by Indian ponies, a white one
lame in one fore foot, and a bay one. Buffalo
robes in profusion softened the seats. At a point
about ten miles distant he drove his team close
up to the creek, took a mail sack on his back,
and crossed the creek on a log to a sod house among
the small trees on the other bank. It was the Wood-
ville post office. The next stop was among a few
houses where South Bend, Indiana, people had located a town near a mill site and named it St. Edward. Adam Smith lived on the second bottom land
about a mile away. We were left with him and
he cordially welcomed us.

Land inspection began next morning. The four
of us in a jump-seat buggy drawn by one horse,
started out to see the land. We had been accustomed to seeing prairie land level and were surprised
to find that while this land was what was called
gently rolling, it looked like quite hilly land to us.
That night Mr. Smith's family, who had moved in
high society in the east, served a fine dinner in
courses of which one was venison, a dish we were
not accustomed to. The celebrated grade wagon
road was in process of construction and Thomas
Wilkinson, one of the county commissioners, was
accompanying the grader to see that the work was
done right. He was a leader among the settlers.

Mr. Smith had hired a team of an Irish neighbor
to take the dinner baskets and the commissioner

to accompany the road grader on a trip of several miles. The team did not return as soon as the old Irishman expected it would and he abused Mr. Smith shamefully, all of which Mr. Smith overlooked and successfully soothed his irate neighbor.

Mr. Smith continued showing us land priced at $2.50 to $4.00 an acre till the boys who accompanied me were cloyed, and pronounced it all too hilly. I advised if he had better land that he show it. He drove toward the county seat and showed some $5.00 an acre land that I later bought. It was a land of magnificent distances and few obstructions and he showed me a mile long strip for a half mile quarter section. He had no higher priced land and I bought 160 acres. I asked that he cut a forty acre strip off the quarter section that was bottom land that I feared would be too springy and give me forty acres on a section cornering the quarter. The forty acres was a magnificent building place with a view of the beautiful valley for many miles. He agreed to do this but assured me the people valued the bottom land higher than the rest. He gave me a discount of 40 per cent for cash, making the land $3.00 an acre. I reconsidered the matter during the winter and bought the forty acre strip of bottom land I had cut off from the 160 and 75 acres that belonged with the forty acre building place and extending into the valley. On this I got a discount of fifty per cent, paying $2.50 an acre cash. Four hundred dollars an acre was offered and refused for ground lying alongside this land during the inflation period following the World War.

We drove on to Albion, the county seat, and ate supper. A cold rain had set in and farmers had come in and filled the only livery stable with their horses. None of them would give way to let Mr. Smith feed his horse. They showed the jealous disposition of the homesteader toward those who seemed in easier circumstances than they were.

That night a heavy rain fell and the next day we started on the return trip without the others buying land. It was a marvelous vacation for me and I saw more new things than I would have seen on a journey to Europe.

I resumed the grind of my profession and the trail having been blazed to Boone county, Nebraska, others began to visit the same place. Adam Smith visited us occasionally to sell land. He was a finished real estate man and a fine promoter and his word was good. He arranged with a lawyer to sell his land for a commission. It happened that an old man who had lived long in Indiana and had got into debt on his light soil rough farm, met this lawyer. He listened to a trade proposition whereby he took 160 acres of Adam Smith's hilliest unimproved land on the deal for $6,400.00. I could have bought the whole 160 acres for $288.00 cash.

He made a visit of inspection to Nebraska and noted the excellent soil and promising conditions, and decided that he had not been beaten in the trade, regardless of the boost that had been given the Nebraska land. He returned home and moved to Nebraska with his whole tribe and never seemed to regret it.

An Indiana man had employed me as physician for his family consisting of himself, wife and five children. They had suffered much from malaria. He was in my office on the occasion of one of Adam

Smith's visits and heard the rosy recital of the advantages offered in Nebraska, and proposed that I send him out to rent my land. I agreed to it and made a contract with him to break 120 acres of the land, crop it to wheat and give me a third of the crop, delivered at market. I was to pay for the breaking. I had a good door and two windows framed for him at a local shop and boards and rafters to cover a sod house, and the sod for the house was on the land. He loaded a pair of horses and personal belongings into a car, taking a young single man along, to take care of the stock, and with his family on a passenger train set out for the west. He broke 80 acres of land that year and next spring sowed it to spring wheat and surprised me by sending a good stiff check for my rent share after he marketed the crop.

The check interested me and I concluded to make another inspection of Nebraska. This time I was accompanied by my oldest brother who had pioneered Indiana with my father. A railroad had just been built to the county seat four miles distant from my land and much improvement in the country was noted. My brother was greatly pleased with the opportunities for a young man there and expressed himself, that if younger, he would go there at once.

We found that my renter had made a good sod house and the material I had supplied him with helped make a presentable home. He plastered the inside walls with clay, dug a well, and made a big sod stable with a brush and hay roof. His family was hospitable and we stayed over night with them. There were eight in his family and we made ten. We were given one of the two beds and I was soon

asleep. Soon the bed bugs began to bite and the
fleas made themselves at home, and brother could
not sleep. The two family dogs, one a bird dog
and the other a hound, had taken night quarters
under our bed. A sudden alarm outdoors aroused
them up hurriedly and as they raised up under the
bed they gave a great boost to the mattress and
the rest of the night was sleepless for brother.

I returned to Indiana and decided to move to
Nebraska myself. Every argument imaginable was
made to induce me to abandon the plan. All of our
relatives seemed to think they would never see us
again. My nearest neighbor said he would not give
my practice for the entire state of Nebraska. He
warned against all the ills he had ever heard of,
Indians, cowboys, horse thieves, blizzards in winter
and cyclones in summer, drouths, hot winds, grasshoppers, and rattlesnakes. He contended that it
was a shame to expose my wife to all such evils
but he cared less for me because I was so obstinate
that I would not admit of any of those ills when
I met them.

I sold my practice and April 18, 1881, after a
goodby visit to our relatives, loaded a car with my
two driving horses and buggy, a farm team and
all our personal property. My wife's brother had
just attained his majority and went along and rode
with the stock. My wife, four year old boy and myself went by passenger train. Delays on the road
because of high water held back the car which we
overtook at Fremont, Nebraska, and we left the
train at Columbus. The car had been billed to
Albion, and freight prepaid, but as Jay Gould's new
bridge across the Loup river had gone out we

could get no farther than Columbus. Next day we unloaded our car. I hired two teams with hay racks on wagons and with our team, and my family in our buggy, we got several miles on the road and stayed over night. The water was high in all streams and the bridge across Beaver creek at Genoa was reported unsafe. The heavy wagons took a road over the hills and did not arrive at our farm till nightfall next day. We drove directly up the Adam Smith grade road till we reached the unsafe bridge, when my family walked over the bridge, and I drew the buggy across by hand and then led the horses over. It is worthy of note that the bridge was afterward used for heavy loads all summer.

We reached our farm at noon and found the family only waiting our arrival to move to a homestead they had taken for themselves. My wife became unhappy for the first time when she saw bed bugs racing up the walls. That night the family of eight and our family of four and the two men I had hired somehow passed the night in that soddy. The family moved to their own place next day. My wife had a good thick white-wash made and plastered on the walls and effectually got rid of the bugs. Had there not been a board roof to the house, getting rid of the bed bugs would have been impossible.

I set about building a new frame house at once and a good four-room dwelling with closets was made on a brick wall with cellar, house sided, sheeted, papered, plastered, painted outside and inside, a brick well, and a cistern made. By active pushing, the house was ready to occupy early in June. I was materially urged to make haste because of our experiences. We had a good sod house but the joints between the layer of sods on the roof required a renewal of fine clay occasionally to keep rain water from trickling through, though we did not know this. We laid a board floor in the end of the room back from the stove and by hanging a curtain in the middle had two sleeping rooms where privacy could be observed. When it rained, the roof leaked the dirty water onto our bed and I would wake up with water running through my hair, and had to put dishes and water proof buggy curtains on the bed to catch the water. My books were safely boxed and in the dryest place in the room. Had our neighbors, who enjoyed our experiences, told us to put a little loose dirt on the cracks in the roof we would have lived dry. We used that building for a grain house for a good while afterward.

Our renter had a sod stable about 35 feet long. When he moved away he took with him the poles and brush that held the straw roof on. I replaced it with a peak board roof and cut an opening in the north wall to run my buggy in. I did not realize that the prevailing strong winds came from the northwest. Partitions were made of boards to divide one end into four stalls for horses. One day a strong northwest wind brought a heavy shower accompanied by some hail. Realizing that there might be trouble at the stable, my brother-in-law and myself went inside with the horses. I took a position between the horses. Soon the wind got under the roof and after a few boosts it went high in the air like a reversed umbrella taking the stalls with it and smeared the roof for forty rods over the prairie. My wife came to the door to see what had

become of her men folks and the water rushed in
as she opened the door. When she saw the condition of the stable, she was fearful that she had
lost her male relatives. These experiences in moving were incidental to hundreds of people who moved
household goods by railroad.

By July we were settled in our farm home which
was four miles southeast of Albion, the principal
town in that part of the state. Many of those engaged in business or the professions lived on farms
near the town. This county, taken as a unit, resembled the state in the different nationalities comprising homesteaders. One county might contain
people of the same nationality speaking the same
language. In one county the early homesteaders
might largely be Germans, or Irish or Bohemians or
Swedes or native Americans but Boone county had
them all. They colonized precincts by accretion as
counties in other places were occupied by people
speaking the same language. In time, in both county
and state, the universal language came to be English. A diversity of language came to influence
church congregations. Usually towns the size of
Albion supported four churches but Albion had
eight. Besides there were many who worshipped
with no denomination.

After a few years so many business opportunities
opened up that I ceased to answer professional
calls, though I kept in touch with the physician's
work, performed post mortem examinations, met
others in council and performed an occasional surgical operation, served as secretary of the U. S. Pension Examining Board in about 400 examinations
and made examinations for life insurance; but I was

a supernumerary in the profession. I became somewhat versatile in my occupation and engaged in
drug and mercantile business, conducted grain raising and fattening cattle and hogs for market,
served as county commissioner and postmaster at
Albion and many local positions.

Boone county was ten years old when we went
there to live. The Pawnee Indians had been moved
from their reservation joining this county on the
south to the Indian Territory, later Oklahoma, and
a branch of the Union Pacific railroad was serving
the needs of transportation. No Indians, except
members of the Omaha tribe, ever paid the county
a visit after we made our home there. Many evi-
dences of their former occupancy remained and
graves were sometimes uncovered. Skeletons of several human beings were uncovered on a high point
of a hill standing out into the valley near Albion.
They were no doubt Indian bones but no one knew
what tribe they belonged to or when buried.

Our neighborhood people were largely from eastern towns who had emigrated to Nebraska to secure
cheap land and become farmers. They were a fine
class of people. The first settlers were living in
frame houses on the valley land and the later comers
lived in sod houses on the high land. Social gatherings were common and the lunches of fried chicken,
cake and delicacies, served to guests in those primitive homes, could not have been excelled anywhere.
The sod school house had given way to a small frame
building just before we arrived. The school district
was the fourth one organized in the county and the
best able to support a good school of any district
in the county. With a number of taxable farms,

a strip of railroad, and much personal property, the school levy was only two mills; but they had been sparing of the length of the school terms.

I was made a member of the school board and at once began to agitate the employing of a higher qualified teacher and a former Chicago teacher was secured for a time, at a good salary, and a nine month school term was held. It proved so satisfactory that the patrons approved a still longer term and decided to build the school house larger. This house became the public hall for all entertainments, social gatherings, Sunday School and religious services. I served them as chorister. A family living in a sod house contracted malignant diphtheria and a strong twelve year old girl died after a short illness. She retained her consciousness to the last although her flesh was in a gangrenous condition. The funeral was held in the one room home. The superintendent of the Sunday School who was also a Methodist class leader, read a chapter from the Bible and offered prayer, and I led the singing assisted by the few women who ventured into the house. The girl was buried in the garden. The men prudently remained out of doors to avoid the infection.

I believe in prayer but believe that it should be a direct supplication accompanied by faith. I recall one that seemed to me to lack force, and to have been misdirected by an excited minister. A prominent citizen living in a distant town of the county, an excellent and religious man of 72 years, had been a frequent visitor at the office of my newspaper. He seemed to approve my editorial work and my personally sociable treatment of visitors. His son-in-law was a leading physician of our town. The old gentleman developed a cancer on his hand that would not yield to treatment and amputation of the hand was advised. The patient would not listen to having any other surgeon in the state operate but insisted that I must do it. I consented and with two other doctors went to the old man's home in the other town. I let the others decide who would administer the anaesthetic and attend the other details. The elderly pastor of the family church, a Civil war veteran, was asked to invoke Divine help before the ordeal began. He appeared to be nervous and excited. He earnestly petitioned for Divine aid and support for all members of the family, for the assistants and myself and that my hand might be strengthened and be firm and fail me not during what he pronounced, a critical operation. But he entirely overlooked the patient who was to be operated on, who in my opinion should have been the chief beneficiary and first in the good pastor's thoughts. There were critics who insisted that the old gentleman knew his business. The operation that took the hand and part of the arm gave the patient freedom for about two years when it appeared in his arm pit and the end soon came.

CHAPTER IV

The Ways of the Country

"Far from the madding crowd's ignoble strife
Their sober wishes never learned to stray;
Along the cool sequestered vale of life
They kept the noiseless tenor of their way."
—*Gray*.

 MADE my home at Albion, in Boone county, for many years. Boone county was located centrally in the grain producing, eastern part of the state. The homesteaders and settlers took the untilled prairie from the territorial settlers and kept it thirty years and delivered it to their successors as a finished product, fit for a place among the sisterhood of the states composing our great nation. This county was all in the grain belt except two townships in the northwestern corner that was the extreme southeastern point of the sandhill cattle range. The people were composed of different nationalities who colonized the county by accretion, in the matter of nationality, and made the county the unit, as the people in different counties recognized the state as the unit for all counties. Albion, the county seat, having the first railroad, became the receiving and shipping point for freight for several counties adjacent. Among them were Wheeler and Greeley counties.

The first Boone county settler filed on a homestead claim near Albion in April, 1871. A party of men came from Columbus, Nebraska, and several filings were made in rapid succession. Four of them entered into an agreement with Columbus people to grub stake them, and give material for a house, and all pool their interests. Accordingly a story and a half frame house was built on a corner stake on the edge of what is now Albion, and four claims of 160 acres each, entered the pool. The pool was later dissolved and the undertaking declared a failure. A homesteader who filed on what was later a part of the town site, and lived on it till his death many years later, also owned a tract of timber lying on each side of the creek adjoining the town on the northwest. This he willed to the town for a park. The town secured the old pioneer frame house and moved it to the park where it will remain as a monument to the first settlers.

A widow woman named Rice was the first woman settler to file a homestead claim in the county. Eventually her claim was made the county seat by act of the legislature. For some time the main part of the pioneer house was occupied by twelve men who had the main floor and attic and Mrs. Rice had a small lean-to on the side of the building where she lived and cooked for the men. It also served as a hotel to feed and shelter land seekers inspecting the country. It was built a few rods south of Beaver creek.

The post office was located in Albert Dresser's dugout a half mile north on the north side of the creek. About this time a unique character appeared on the scene with his wife and three little boys. They came directly from England where they had lived in a town and knew nothing about either English or American farming and in such a new country and homestead kind of farming, they were simply infants under the care of a merciful Heavenly Father. They were penniless, but he could do some kinds of work that the settlers could not do and was a likeable man. His name was J. W. Turner and he afterwards put out an interesting book reciting their experiences. At first they were surprised that there were no public bakeries and his wife did not know how to make bread. He took a homestead claim a short distance north and prepared to make a sod house. As a temporary dwelling place while making his sod house, he dug a square hole in the side of a bank by a small creek and brought his effects from Columbus and started to live there, with a bed blanket for a roof covering. A big rain came up and flooded the little valley and swept them out of their hole in the bank, and all their property, his wife's English hat and all, went down stream, and they narrowly escaped with their lives.

These settlers lived near the Pawnee Indian agency but were not often molested by them. The Pawnees did not go far from the agency, fearing that a lurking war party of Sioux would be lying in wait for them. The Sioux came by to harass the Pawnees but were afraid of reprisals if they disturbed the white settlers. Occasionally the Sioux would seize a pig or calf for food, but seldom stole anything else.

Judge J. Watson Riley, who had been a pioneer county judge, lived three miles southeast of Albion. He told me that he once had a bad scare when a Sioux war party crossed the valley between his place and town. They had been on a marauding expedition against the Pawnees and were hurriedly

retreating. One of the young Riley boys was plowing near where the Indians had to pass. Mr. Riley
feared that they would attack the boy, or their dog
would attack the Indians and attract them to the
boy. He knew that an attack would result in certain death for his family and himself but he took
a position in his grove with a long range rifle intending to fire on the Indians at the first hostile
demonstration against the boy. Happily they passed
by, intent on putting distance between them and
their pursuers whom they had thrown off the track
by an abrupt turn in direction.

The cheap land induced several capitalists in Chicago and Detroit to buy large tracts of land and
made ranches that were operated at a loss, but the
advance in land values eventually made it a profitable investment. The opulent owners of the ranches
helped the country by introducing good live stock.
One prominent Chicago man secured a valuable tract
comprising grain land, choice wild hay land, and
excellent pasture land with shade trees and good
water. It was ideal in all ways. He sent his
brother-in-law to manage the place. This man incurred great loss by his unwise management and
the ranch was finally sold. Many cattle and hogs
were grain fattened on the place during its active
days. It was called Williamsdale Ranch. The manager disposed of the manure from the feed yard by
having men use road scrapers to move it to a level
place across the road and pile it in a long high hill,
where it remained a monument to the waste of fer-
tilizer. One hot July day he had a carload of big
fat hogs to move to the shipping station some miles
distant. He undertook to make them walk and

nearly all died on the way from overheating. Other dude ranches were conducted with the same kind of losses from bad management till the capitalists that owned them accepted Benjamin Franklin's motto that,

> "He, who by the plow would thrive,
> Must himself hold the plow, or drive."

Productive activities up to 1896 found agriculture in the new state the fundamental occupation. At that time the meat packing industry took the lead in Nebraska manufactures. To bring about this result, grain farming by the first settlers, especially the first year's cropping of spring wheat, had to give way to cattle and swine raising.

Naturally flour milling followed the production of wheat on the newly cultivated land. The first mill recorded as operating in the territory was erected in Richardson county in 1850. The first mills were operated by water power and usually consisted of two-burr run of mill stones, one for wheat and the other for corn. Buckwheat and rye flour were produced on either run of burrs. It is recorded that flour milling stood first in manufactures in the young state in 1870. At the close of the first thirty years of statehood in 1897 the meat packing industry passed flour milling, and butter and dairy products came close behind.

The sandhill country and the buffalo ranges of western Nebraska furnished the first supplies of fat cattle to the packing houses that were for the greater part, located at Missouri river points. The short grass sections produced gramma and buffalo grass naturally. The short buffalo grass ripened and retained its vitamins and nourishing properties as it shrank into thin fine blades of dried grass. A winter pasture of this grass could hardly be considered of value by a person not familiar with it. The ground would be plainly visible yet the dried grass was so nourishing that cattle came to the packing houses in March from those pastures as fat as though corn fed in the yards in the grain raising section. Many of the range cattle and sheep from the mountains were shipped into eastern Nebraska in October to be finished on the corn surplus found there.

The mode of feeding cattle varied from the first attempts. Little shelter was provided for cattle on the range. The first grain feeders tried the no-shelter plan in eastern Nebraska in finishing cattle for the packing houses. Many times a thousand cattle, usually two and three year old steers, were seen during the early eighties confined in an open lot, exposed to the winter winds and snow and piercing cold without shelter except for a row of small trees from which the leaves had fallen. They were fed abundantly with corn and supplied with water but the ice water they were offered did not appeal to them with a twenty below temperature. It was seldom that this kind of feeding was profitable.

Wisdom and experience brought about better feeding methods when protecting sheds were provided, water warmed with tank heaters, corn and forage supplied in abundance with hogs to follow the cattle to pick up the waste. The hogs were the scavengers and made the profit in a feed lot, and there were no left over buffalo chips in a feed lot.

Any kind of forage, wild hay, alfalfa, or straw was stacked in the yards with a strong fence around it but so arranged that the cattle could eat forage at will and not trample it under foot. Cattle taken off grass were fed snapped corn till along in December when they had become accustomed to a big ration of grain. The shell corn or chop corn was supplied them on broad tables of convenient height and they were fed daily. An improvement was a small house built on the middle of the feed tables, bunks they were called, that would hold about 600 bushels of corn and run down through a crack at the bottom onto the bunk so that cattle fed themselves.

The country flouring mills sometimes gathered herds of cattle and hogs and fed the mill bran and shorts as produced. One mill yarded 220 head of cattle and 200 hogs in October and fed them out till the next May, shipping out as the stock matured. At first snap corn was fed them, which made both grain and roughness. Then corn was ground coarse in the mill and taken to the yards well mixed with bran and placed on the feed bunks three times a day. Wild hay, straw, flax straw and any kind of rough forage was placed before them. One man easily took care of the entire lot and the feeding venture proved profitable.

Few sheep were raised in eastern Nebraska but in the extreme west large herds were pastured and either shipped east in the fall for a corn finish or left on the range till matured and then sent directly to the slaughter houses at Omaha. Sheep did very well on the ranges regardless of the cold, but if snow came they suffered for lack of pasturage because it was covered up. The owner was then obliged to scatter corn on the ground for them to gather up. White corn that is prized for feeding yard use, would be rejected by sheep men because its color made it hard for the sheep to see it in the snow, so yellow or dark corn brought a premium when sold to sheep ranchers.

Naturally dairying followed flour milling and live stock fattening the meat packing industry. The cheap pasturage seemed ideal for the production of milk and butter. Creameries began to spring up. The first commercial creamery noted in the state was one at Waterloo, Nebraska, a point west of Omaha where the Union Pacific railroad crossed the Elkhorn river. It was established in 1871. As farm production became greater than could find a remunerative market, farmers staged political uprisings at different times and sought to bring relief by the farmers alliance and populist movements. Farm made butter, lacking improved methods in making, and sanitary care before marketing, was little better than rancid grease when it reached a buyer and only brought producers six cents a pound.

It was then that creameries were established to gather the milk from the farms and separate the cream and churn the butter at some nearby railway station. Merchants in town would finance milk routes to gather the milk from the farms, or farmers themselves would bring it in and be given back the milk from which the butter fat had been separated. Then followed the individual farm separators and milk no longer left the farm after the cream had been marketed. Cheese factories sometimes tried to use the milk but they did not prove as successful as the creameries.

A country town creamery. This creamery took in an average of 15,000 lbs. of the farmers' milk daily and separated the butterfat from the milk and churned it and sent the butter to market. It was the forerunner of the modern family cream separator. Sometimes the milk was gathered by the creamery by establishing routes among the farmers to whom they lent milk cans. As a rule the farmers brought in the milk themselves early in the morning and were given the separated milk to feed pigs and calves.

Illustrating hundreds of milling plants in Nebraska country towns. At one time it was the principal Nebraska industry next to agriculture. Such milling plants usually sold flour, mill feed and grain to customers at the door and shipped the surplus. They also bought and shipped grain and sold coal. As a help to local business they stored flour for the farmers who came to town to get a sack of flour and lingered to patronize the stores.

The Homestead Act was a law passed by Congress to give free homes to people who would occupy and develop the unimproved lands belonging to the United States Government. The Homestead Act provided that an actual settler who would occupy and cultivate 160 acres of the public domain for five years, would receive a government deed to the land. The only other expense to him was the payment of a nominal fee for filing on the land and another when he made proof of having complied with the law. Concessions were made to single persons, men or women, to permit absence from the land for employment or on business, but the family of a married person must actually occupy the land. It is worthy of note that the first homestead taken under the act was 160 acres in southeastern Nebraska. A homesteader could prove up on his claim at any time by paying $1.25 an acre for it but most homesteaders chose to occupy the land principally because they lacked means for buying it. A timber claim might be taken without actual residence but a certain amount of the land must be planted to forest trees and compliance with the requirements for eight years gave a government patent to the settler who paid the usual filing and proving up fee. Only one quarter in each section could be taken under the timber claim act. Nebraska state encouraged tree planting by making land so planted free of taxes.

Vast bodies of land was given railroads to help them construct their lines. It was allowed them in alternate sections, the other ones being open to homesteaders or reserved, two sections in each township for the support of schools. These two sections

known as school sections were taken from the allotment to the states by the United States Government
for educational purposes. The railroad land was sold
to settlers or speculators at very low prices and on
very liberal terms. Prices per acre usually ranged
between $2.25 and $5.00 with discount for cash, or
as long as ten years time with no principal payment
for four years, and interest at six per cent per
annum.

Already the hand writing was seen on the wall
warning that farm relief must come from intensive
farming, with the Nebraska cow and hen the foundation of agricultural prosperity.

Little grain was ever harvested in Nebraska by
the hand cradle and hand rake method that pioneers
in the timber countries of the middle west had to
use. The harvester that cut the grain and elevated
it for two men standing on the machine to bind with
straw, was the Nebraska primitive harvester. The
best farm implements of the times were available
for the sod house period if the settler but paid the
price. Many a homesteader lost his valuable 160 acre
farm by reason of a mortgage placed on it to buy
farm machinery that was ruined by standing out
the entire year in a sunflower cluster for its only
shelter.

Typical of most counties in the grain section of
Nebraska, Boone county decided that it must have
an agricultural association and hold annual fairs.
As a rule all such movements were started and
financed by the town people, and most of the work
done by them, while the farmers were expected to
provide the exhibits of farm products and live stock.
Such a county fair was organized at Albion for

Boone county and became one of the undisputedly largest county fairs in the west. It held its first meeting in 1886. The secretary, by usage, was the general manager. The first and second secretaries each held office three years. I was drafted for the third secretary and held the place six years. Times began to be hard in 1892 and the great financial panic struck the country in 1893. In 1894 the state had an entire crop failure caused by drouth and hot winds. Crops were good the succeeding years but all the primitive live stock had been taken from the country and the immense crops of corn only brought the farmers nine to eleven cents a bushel. My predecessors left a big fair debt for me to wrestle with. Our fair executive board consisted of W. A. Poynter, president, and later governor of the state; S. S. Hadley, treasurer and representative of the eastern capitalists, who had bought large tracts of land; and myself as secretary. The other two loyally supported me and made it possible for me to do the work by giving me free rein. I worked without pay and had my employes work for the fair for which I was not paid. That policy got a great deal of free work for the fair. The fair was the one thing that harmonized and united all classes of our people.

The fair developed roadsters, draft horses and high grade cattle and hogs. The loss of crop in 1894 proved to be a benefit to the country. The spavined and blemished breeding stock of early days was all taken out of the country, and the weeds were killed by the 1894 drouth. Farmers made a start in 1895 on clean ground for crops, and the best pure bred horses, cattle and hogs in the world replaced the worthless homesteader stock. The town people guaranteed payment for a car load of seed oats furnished by the Chicago board of trade and divided it out into 20 bushel lots to farmers who became wealthy in a few years. Money was so scarce that one year there were 37 entries of wild plum jelly exhibited at the fair. The first prize was 35 cents and the second a diploma. It was difficult under such conditions to keep the fair going but at the close of 1897 I relinquished the office with all debts paid and a few dollars in the treasury. With a new era at hand and a live organization, the fair went on to great prosperity and functioned for the good of its own and neighboring counties.

CHAPTER V

A Sod House Home

"Mid pleasures and palaces though we may roam,
Be it ever so humble, there's no place like home."
—*Payne.*

NEBRASKA territorial homesteader's house was made of logs in a limited favored section where timber was available, but the typical Nebraska homesteader almost invariably made his home of sod or dug a hole into the side of a hill or ravine. The "dugout" might be wholly excavated or excavated with an open top that was covered over with a roofing of logs, brush, prairie hay and sods with a door and possibly a window in the end fronting on a ravine.

A more pretentious dwelling was made wholly above ground. A variation, and variations were many, might be to excavate a foot or two below the surface for the inside of the building and thus reduce the height of the side walls. Nebraska homesteaders did not use sun burned bricks, gumbo or make mud houses. Adobe houses were found nearer the Mexican border south, and southwest. The sides of a real Nebraska homesteader's habitation were made of real good fertile Nebraska loamy, clayey earth. It was seldom called a "Doby" but might be called a Nebraska marble or brick house, a soddy, or a dugout.

A homesteader usually drove his prairie schooner onto the quarter section of land he had filed his claim upon and camped. If he had any money after paying the filing fees on his homestead claim he was fortunate. But he had health, strength, a young wife and perhaps children, a team of horses and wagon, and the wagon was their home for a time. As soon as possible he located a building place. If he proposed to make a dugout, he found a favorable ravine, or draw as they were called, where he could dig out into the bank and have an east front outlook. A board door was framed and set up with a small window by its side. If the dugout was wholly under ground little more than the excavation was required except to fill in around the door frames and dig a hole for a stove pipe out through the top of the hill.

I have had the experience while making my rounds as a physician, to discover a stove pipe protruding from the ground surrounded by prairie grass. An inspection would reveal a door on the side of the ravine. I visited exactly such a dugout once when I hired the homesteader's wife to go home with me to do some work for our family. The excavation was about fourteen feet wide and sixteen feet dug into a hillside. A cook stove, bed, milk safe and a few other articles sufficed for the man and his wife and five children. The dirt floor had become uneven with depressions made by sweeping. The milk safe was blocked up one side to keep it from tipping over. A pan of milk rested on top of the safe. The woman stepped against it and disturbed the pan of milk so that it tipped off and as luck would have it, it spilled down her neck. She was a big, tall, bony woman, very lightly clad and the milk gave her a thorough drenching.

This particular home had a pig pen near by. Its arrangement was born of necessity. Without fencing or hog house at his command, the homesteader had dug a hole in the ground so deep, and with such steep sides that a brood of pigs occupied it without being able to escape. This homesteader hauled water for household use in his wagon from an older place that possessed a well that was located a mile and a half away.

Another way of making a dugout was made mandatory where the hill was not high enough to leave a natural roof or the ravine was too shallow so an artificial roof had to be prepared. This was made by placing tree logs across the top of the cavity, then a layer of brush, then coarse hay and lastly sods and dirt completed the cover. Through this the stove pipe protruded. This roof had to be guarded to keep stray livestock from falling through it onto the family underneath.

The more pretentious sod houses followed a common plan of a building sixteen feet wide on outside and of variable length. A common house would be twenty feet long but some of them were longer, depending upon the resources of the builder.

The first step in making a new home would be to select the location and then choose the best low spot where the sod would be thickest and strongest. A breaking plow was used to turn over furrows on about half an acre of ground, using care to make the furrows of even width and thickness so that the home wall would rise evenly. A spade was used to cut the furrow into sod bricks about three feet long. A float made of planks or the forks of a tree or even the wagon drawn by horses or oxen, was used to transport the sod bricks to the building place. The first layer in the wall was made by placing three foot-wide bricks side by side around the foundation except where the door would be located, carefully breaking joints. When the first row was placed, the cracks were filled with fine dirt and two more layers placed on top, all the time breaking joints as a brick layer breaks joints. Every third course was laid crosswise of the others to bind them together. This process was followed till the walls were high enough to take the roof. A door frame had been set on the ground and built around with sods and two window frames placed higher up in the wall, one by the door and the other opposite on the other side of the house. The wall was then carefully trimmed to symmetrical proportions by the use of a sharp spade.

The roof was the next to be considered. The most expensive soddies were made with a framed roof with a ridge peak in the middle, using 2x4 dimension stuff for rafters set on a 2x6 plate on the wall. Sheeting was nailed on the rafters and tar paper spread over the sheeting boards. This was again covered with sods somewhat thinner than the sods used for side walls. These were laid smoothly and the cracks filled with fine clay dirt. Such a roof would shed water very well but the dirt filling between cracks in the sods required renewing as the rains carried it away. The gable ends of the building might be boarded up, otherwise they were sodded up as the side walls had been.

A board floor might be laid and the inside side walls plastered up with the gray colored clay dug from below the black surface dirt, made a very presentable wall when finished. With doors and windows in place such a home with furniture brought from the old home in the east, with perhaps a carpet on the floor and an organ or piano and good furniture, a nice home would have been established that looked well inside even if it was very plain on the outside. But this is a roseate picture of the very few homes where the settler had brought some money with him. The house wall being three feet thick made a surprisingly comfortable home, being warm in winter and cool in summer.

But the settler might not have any money with which to buy boards yet must have a home to shelter his family. He followed the plan used in making the more pretentious sod house as far as he could and the walls were not much unlike the better ones. The roof was the difficult thing to provide and the most of the sod house homesteaders made the roof of crooked limbs, brush, coarse prairie hay and a thick covering of sod and dirt. To hold up such a load a forked tree was planted in each end of the house and a ridge pole log placed from one gable to the other resting in the forks. From the ridge pole to the walls, poles and limbs were laid. They were wonderfully crooked limbs but they covered a home for the homesteader and his family, and were comfortable, even if less prepossessing than the home of the neighbor who could afford a lumber roof to his "soddy."

The question of heating those sod houses and dugouts was not a serious one regardless of the fact that coal was not easy to get. The Rock Springs

coal from Wyoming mines was all that eastern Nebraska was supplied with well up into the eighties.
The Rock Springs coal mines were owned by the
Union Pacific railroad and they supplied all their
stations at a uniform price. It did not interest the
primal settlers much because they had no money
with which to buy coal. But in the bottom of draws
and ravines sunflowers and rosin weeds grew luxu-
riantly and when dried after the frost came in the
fall, would produce quite a bit of heat when fed
into the family cook stove, or would make a hasty
fire to cook a meal. Sometimes sumach or plum
shrubs would be found and every stick that could
be made to burn was made use of. A very common
fuel, and one always available, was the wild prairie
hay. The ground not under cultivation produced
an excellent prairie hay. A sod house could easily
be warmed by twisting the prairie hay into a close
hard rope and crowding it into the cook stove side
door. A drawback to this fuel was the hay littered
about, and some smoke came from the open stove
door. The fireman had a steady job but a great
deal of heat was developed. Eastern Nebraska
homesteaders made little use of buffalo chips.

As the settlers prospered and began to raise sod
corn or big fields of cultivated corn, much corn was
used for fuel. At times during the nineties, when
booster corn crops alternated with crop failures,
corn was cheaper fuel than to sell it for nine cents
a bushel and buy coal. Corn made a good fire and
would keep any house warm. Then the cobs left
after shelling made a splendid clean fuel, good summer and winter. The prosperous farmer in after
years, shelling several thousand bushels of corn for

market or for his feed lot, required very little coal
to help the cobs heat any kind of house during the
coldest winter weather.

Being short of funds and lacking credit at the
store, the homesteader's family went without gro-
ceries, meat, pork and milk for several years. The
food supply was a difficult one and the settlers were
for long periods undernourished. Pigs and cows,
where in a few years they were shipped out by the
thousand, were very scarce. Even after occupying
the claim several years, at times the family was reduced to a diet of potatoes without pork, milk or
butter to make them palatable. Sometimes such
things could be secured by working for a neighbor,
but that source was not dependable.

Adam Smith, of whom I bought my land, settled
the want of common work horses by buying street
car horses in Chicago that had become unservice-
able because their feet became sore pounding the
pavement. In the beginning they were good heavy
horses, but street car wear and tear stiffened them
and broke and bruised their feet till they were useless for drawing street cars, hence a liability in the
city where they could not be used. Mr. Smith
bought them very cheap and turned them loose to
run on soft earth and they soon regained their use-
fulness and the settlers bought them at reasonable
prices on time and they did good service.

The first settler to file on government land under
the National Homestead Act made his choice of 160
acres in southeastern Nebraska. The total expense
of filing on a 160 acre tract of government land and
"proving up" after the expiration of five years,
amounted to about ten cents an acre but many of

the pioneer settlers were so lacking in money that
they had to wait till they could secure money enough
to pay the first filing fees. Of course someone else
might file on the tract the settler had chosen and
was holding only as a squatter. But other homesteaders always sympathized with the squatter and
the claim jumpers safety was always in jeopardy.
As a matter of fact, the settler who had difficulty
in raising his homestead filing fee sometimes had
to be satisfied with the poorest kind of sod house.
Some of them might lack the door and windows and
have the entire roof covered with sods that carried
great growths of sunflowers and grass on the roof.
A homesteader might "commute" on his land after
a period of residence on it and buy it at government price or he might take a preemption claim
and buy the land under the other terms, or he
might take a timber claim and secure the land by
growing trees on it without having to live on it.

Logs and small trees and branches, especially
forked top posts to hold up the ridgepole of the sod
house and a long straight ridge pole log were absolutely necessary, and early settlers found considerable timber areas along the streams and ravines. A
tract of heavily timbered country was found in the
lower Loup river valley and set aside as a reservation for the Pawnee Indians. The settlers for many
miles around made free use of the Indian timber
for finishing material for their sod houses, stock
shelter and fire wood. Of course they could not be
given permission to take the timber but the needs
of the settlers were so well known that the taking
of the timber was winked at by the authorities.

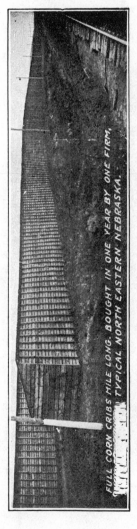

FULL CORN CRIBS MILE LONG. BOUGHT IN ONE YEAR BY ONE FIRM, TYPICAL NORTH EASTERN NEBRASKA.

These corn cribs were full of ear corn and bought in one season. The picture was taken from a photograph. The cribs are eight feet wide and correspondingly high. They were in three rows but if connected together in one crib would be a mile long. Later the corn was shelled and shipped in freight cars to market. In time, very little ear corn was marketed by the farmers and the amount of shell corn shipped out was greatly restricted. The corn was used on the farm for fattening cattle, hogs and sheep and as farmers would say, shipped on the hoof.

A good reproduction of a homesteaders sod house on the uplands. It is true to life. The rolling prairie that has not yet felt the breaking plow, in the background. The boxless wagon, the old topless buggy and the pail that has been used to water the family cow in the foreground. The poles may be seen that carried the clothes line to dry the family washing and the window corner crumbling away near the man and dog. I have visited many such homes, tied my horse to the wagon, and took my medicine kit and visited a patient in the house.

Shelters for livestock were made with sod walls and wood and brush tops, with a hay or straw roofing. A supply of water was imperative. The hilly part of the land away from the streams was cut by many draws or ravines that served to carry the water after rains to the living streams on the bottom lands. Sometimes at points on the tender black earth of the ravine bottoms, holes would be excavated by the water and some of them were large and deep enough to have hidden a goodly sized house. They would remain filled with rain water after the rainfall had been drained away. Before the land was placed under cultivation the water would remain clear. From those cisterns, as they were called, the first homesteaders got their water for all household and stock uses. Presumably the water would be unhealthy but it was not. No instance is recorded of disease following the use of this water that was apparently unsanitary.

As soon as possible the settlers prepared to make wells near their living quarters. Unlike the lands in the middle west where alternate layers of sand, gravel and clay were met in digging wells, the surface of the land over the greater part of eastern Nebraska was composed of "loess," a clayey looking earth identical with the sediment in the Missouri river water. It is not as tenacious as the clay of the middle west and the depth to water depends upon the height of the hill. At a level with the Platte river an underground stream of water is found that furnishes an unfailing supply of water, once the well penetrates through the loess. The depth of wells might vary from 20 to 200 feet, owing to the thickness of the loess deposit.

Well making was simple and the cost small. No stone or gravel would be encountered, no matter how deep the well would be dug. A man with a spade started the open well about 30 inches in diameter. He continued digging as long as he could throw the dirt out of the well then a helper with a windlass joined in the work. Two log posts with forks at the top were set each side of the well. A straight log turned in the forks around which a rope wound and a bucket at lower end would drop into the well to be filled by the well digger and then raised to the surface by the helper by a vigorous use of strong sticks through the end of the log constituting the windlass. The well was dug deeper and deeper and excavated dirt raised to the top of the ground till the sand strata was reached that contained the underground water flow. A board box was set in the watery filled sand at the bottom and the well was complete, with no curbing required except if the settler was extravagant, a curbing three feet deep might be placed around the top where rain and wind might disturb the top soil of the ground. A well windlass and buckets were used to raise the water from the well. These wells endured for many years and many of them were used in later years when a windmill and pump could be secured to make raising the water easier when needs became greater for water for stock. Those dug wells never caved or fell in and the cost of the well was proportionately as low as it was to prepare the land for crops by simply plowing up the sod. Those dug wells all went to the same water level depth. I have seen the loess dirt brought from a 200 foot well produce crops equally with the surface clay after being exposed to the sun for a season.

The homesteader becoming settled and a well dug, began to plan to possess a cow and some pigs. Neither were easy to find for sale by the first homesteaders, and even ten years later it took a long search among the homesteaders to find a couple of pigs or a solitary cow for sale. Then the hardest part was to raise the means to pay for them. Sometimes an extra pig was traded to a neighbor for work and a cow that might be valued at $25.00 changed homes after several shifts in trade.

The pig was given a home by digging a hole in the ground with sides so steep that he could not crawl out, or a sod wall might make him a pen, or he might even go at liberty. The horses and cow were usually sheltered in a straw stable made by planting posts and poles and covering these over with straw at threshing time. Of course in a few years if the settler was prosperous, these primitive improvements gave way to something better. The cow was "staked out" to grass by tying the end of a long rope around her horns and securing the other end by driving an iron picket pin, to which the rope was attached, into the ground. The cow was moved to a new place every day.

Many homesteaders who lived in dugouts or sod houses were not able to own a pig, cow or horse for some time. Perhaps they had secured a yoke of oxen instead of horses and oxen did excellent work breaking the prairie. The oxen were staked out to pasture just as the cow was given a chance to graze.

As improvements were made, a corral fence of wire enclosing a small yard by the stable was provided for the cow. It was some time after the ad-

vent of settlers before they were able to finance the
purchase of barb wire and small pastures were seen
with posts three rods apart and two wires strung
on them. They were but makeshifts for the sug-
stantial fences that came later.

These preliminaries attended to, the plowing of
fire guards on the lines around the quarter section
to keep prairie fires away from the premises, became
imperative. Neglecting to do this, a fire running through the dry grass in fall or spring, might
jump the fire guard and the homesteader would
then have to pay dearly for his neglect or unavoid-
able ill luck, and lose his hay stables, stacks and
possibly the cow or horses with the rest. The next
step would be for a neighbor to circulate a subscrip-
tion paper among the merchants and professional
people in town to help replace the loss.

Then the natural prairie sod must be broken to
prepare for crops. The sod was tough but unlike
Illinois prairie sod was for the most part free from
stones or brush. An occasional prairie weed or
"shoe string root" or pawnee apple root was found.
They would dull the edge of the breaking plow but
by careful attention a plow lay could be kept very
sharp and would easily cut the stiff sod. The point
was of soft steel and had to be taken to a blacksmith frequently to have him heat and beat the
edge down to replace what had been worn or filed
away by the plowman. The sod breaker's technique
was to turn his plow upside down as the point became dull and hold an iron wedge head or an old
ax head under the edge, and pound it down thinner
with a hammer and then smooth the nicks with a
file.

Illinois prairie was broken by a sort of cart carrying a big plow with a wooden mould board and an iron cutting edge. It was drawn by several yoke of oxen and all manner of roots, stones and tough sod was encountered. Hazel brush four feet high was thus turned under and the roots remained to interfere with cultivation for years. Nebraska was favored by lack of obstructions in the ground. At first a sod plow having a long sloping mould board that would cut a furrow 12 or 14 inches wide, was used. Sometimes two horses and sometimes three were required to draw the plow. Improved plows came that were very light and had rods instead of mould board and a cutting surface of 18 or 20 inches that doubled the capacity of a day's breaking, especially if drawn by three horses.

This sod breaking must be done between May 15 and July 1 to get the best results. Broken at other times the sod failed to rot. Much sod corn was planted by chopping a hole with an ax through the sod and dropping the grains of corn in and pressing the dirt around with the foot. Sometimes a sharpened paddle stick was used to make a hole between the furrows or a hand planter was used. It was not a certain crop but sometimes a very good crop was husked from that planting and it was all velvet because no cultivation had been required.

In the fall the sod was backset with the breaking plow and the land was ready to sow to spring wheat any time from February 15 to April 15. The early sowing was best. Sometimes a good crop of flax was grown on the freshly broken sod instead of planting sod corn.

In case the homesteader lacked means to cover his "soddy" with a board roof, or make a floor, it is apparent that his furniture was meager, unless he had brought it with him. Bunks were made by forked poles and slats driven into the sod walls. A table was made the same way. Boxes given them by the town merchants did service as chairs.

An acquaintance told me of his entertainment in a dugout occupied by an old bachelor who had cooked for himself while serving as a soldier during the Civil war. Being invited to go home with John as his guest at dinner after Sunday school, he said that John began dinner by making biscuits. John mixed the dough and flattened small pieces with his hands and laid them on top of the cook stove. Soon they took on a good baking color but it was mostly from the rust and black dirt released by the stove. The outside of the biscuits when served on the table, were streaked and hard, and inside still raw dough. They were but half cooked and went down on the pine board table with a heavy thump. While the biscuits were baking John sliced bacon and put it to sizzling on the stove on a tin plate. That plate and another they found served them for plates to eat from. The coffee was strong and boiled black as the stove pipe. Then came a course of wheat grains, boiled whole, and served with sorghum molasses. No doubt the meals of many homesteaders were more frugal than the one John served his guest.

As a rule the first post offices were located in a convenient dugout or sod house. Strong sticks were driven in the side of a sod house at some point indicated by the housewife and a cracker box from a

store was divided into boxes and used to take care
of the mail. In Boone county the first post office
was in a dugout adjoining Albion, the county seat.
Mr. Dresser, the postmaster, claimed to be the first
settler in Boone county because he rode on the front
seat of the first wagon in which were several men.

In counties composed of valleys and rolling divide
land, the valleys were settled first. Thus the val-
lays showed a bit of improvements when I moved
to Boone county ten years after the first claim had
been taken, but the uplands, or rolling divides, were
being occupied by the first settlers. Forty acres of
the homestead Mr. Dresser took that cost him, when
proved up on, about ten cents an acre, was sold
during the inflation times following the World war
for $500 an acre and there was no improvements
on it except a wire fence and the land was not
adaptable for platting into town lots, being the most
distant part of the farm from town.

Nebraska's first homesteaders were a hardy set
of men and women, mostly under forty years of age.
Many of the men were Civil war veterans. Some
of the first comers were optimistic and stuck by
their land. Some were despondent and discouraged
and home sick. Some were "yellow" and gave up
their fine land and went back to live with their
wives relatives.

CHAPTER VI

Indians—Buffalo—Game

"Lo the poor Indian; whose untutored mind
Sees God in clouds, or hears Him in the wind;
His soul, proud science never taught to stray
Far as the solar walk or milky way."

—*Pope*

HAT is regarded as the most important military movement of Nebraska during territorial times against the Indians was an expedition against a village on the Elkhorn river in Madison county in 1859. From this contact with the Pawnee Indians, the town of Battle Creek took its name. As shown by public records the description of the expedition is brief. Indians were generally numerous and troublesome and the Pawnee tribe had become intolerable nuisances occupying the entire eastern part of the territory north of the Platte river. They constantly harassed the settlers, stealing everything they could lay their hands on, running off stock and committing outrages and in a few instances endangering the lives of the settlers who finally became thoroughly alarmed. For the greater part the marauding Indians at this time lived along the Elkhorn river from fifty to one hundred and fifty miles west of the Missouri river.

About July 1, 1859, settlers began to come into Omaha with reports of Indian outrages and ask for protection. The territorial capital was located at Omaha and there the appeal for help to protect settlers from the Indians was made. Territorial

(72)

Governor Black was in Nebraska City, but J. Sterling Morton was territorial secretary of state, and in Omaha at the time. Under the law Morton would be acting governor when the governor was out of reach. Petitions were circulated in Omaha asking Morton to assume the governorship and start an expedition against the predatory Indians. It was doubtful if the governor was far enough away to warrant Morton acting as governor, but the demand was urgent and Morton was not the man to hesitate for trifles, and he acted promptly and vigorously.

Mr. Morton appealed to the commander of the U. S. troops stationed at Fort Kearney to send a detachment of cavalry to Fontanelle to participate in the expedition. A company of light artillery in Omaha composed of forty men was ordered to mobilize at Fontanelle. They were only citizen militia. General Thayer, afterward governor of the state of Nebraska, claimed to be the head of the military forces of the state, assumed command. Many settlers joined the expedition as volunteers. I was acquainted with a man named Whittaker some years later who was one of the volunteer members of the expedition and he was able to tell a great deal of unrecorded history of the campaign. Before the expedition got under way the governor joined them and assuming that he was entitled to be the commander-in-chief of the expedition by virtue of his office of governor, undertook to assume chief command but General Thayer would not permit it. Many farmers with their horse teams and wagons were requisitioned to carry the supplies and baggage.

Mr. Whittaker said that the army was composed of an unorganized, undisciplined mob, disinclined to take orders from anyone. The detachment of U. S. dragoons of course obeyed their own officers but the dragoons comprised only a small part of the force that left Fontanelle. The artillery militia knew little about discipline and cared less. They were equipped with one small cannon. The main body of the force consisted of volunteer settlers who would not recognize the authority of Thayer or anyone else. Had they been attacked by a band of real warriors they would have been massacred.

Mr. Whittaker said that the most important article in their commissary supplies was whiskey. This was used so liberally that the issue had to be reduced and the army go into camp till whiskey supplies could be brought up. The governor tried to discipline the volunteers but they refused to obey and ridiculed his authority. As they were not enlisted nor bound to stick, it was difficult to keep them from returning home. Finally General Thayer put the governor under restraint and the whiskey supply arriving, the force went forward in a desultory way.

At a point near where the present town of Battle Creek, in Madison county, is located, the Indian village and the main body of Indians were found. Many weird stories have been told about the battle that followed but Mr. Whittaker said that the Indians were not expecting an attack and did not want to fight anyway. They were simply cowardly sneak thieves and degraded mendicants, who would steal anything, beg anything, eat any kind of a dead animal and were only dangerous where white people could offer no resistance. They surrendered at once and the small cannon that the Omaha militia brought with them was discharged several times to impress the Indians with the military power of the white people and also to partially relieve the wish of the Omaha artillery company to burn some powder to reward them for the long march. Then the dragoons fired several volleys to impress the Indians. In this they were joined enthusiastically by the volunteers. One old Indian was killed in a wigwam by mistake, the white warriors thinking the wigwam was empty when they riddled it with gun fire. It was a burlesque battle fought by a burlesque army that influenced the naming of the town of Battle Creek. The demonstration made such an impression on the Indians that they gladly accepted peace and pledged to cease from depredations on the white people.

Regardless of non-resistance on the part of the Indians the expedition was a success in a way because the Indians conducted themselves better for some time after the settlers had returned home. After the peace treaty and the alleged battle, the expedition continued on up the Elkhorn river valley to a point where Oakdale is located and then changed to a southeasterly direction across to Beaver Creek valley in what is Boone county and followed it to the junction of Beaver creek with the Loup river at the present site of Genoa. The government later segregated the remaining Pawnee tribe there on the Loup river and established the agency buildings there. At Columbus the dragoons left the expedition and returned to their quarters at Fort Kearney and the Omaha artillery company and volunteers returned to their homes and disbanded. Their number had been badly decimated by desertions that began when the expedition first started.

It is probable that the danger from those Indians was overrated by the territorial white people. The Pawnees had been a powerful tribe living along both sides of the eastern end of the Platte river, preferably on the south side. Wars with the more aggressive tribes of the plains and their own deterioration by contact with the whites, had broken the morale of the Pawnees. Prevented from securing their share of the game in the buffalo country, by the more warlike Indian tribes, and the destruction of the once abundant game near the section of occupancy by the whites, their courage departed with their food supply. They had been driven out of the South Platte country and crowded into a tract where food sufficient for their support was not available. Those Indians were hungry. A hungry Indian could hardly be classed as the noble red man of romance when his stomach is empty. They would eat things that a hog would not touch. A poisoned coyote or a dog that died of disease they eagerly seized. They annoyed white settlers for food and became sneak thieves from necessity rather than from choice, because the white people had crowded them into a space where they had to go hungry all the time. With their game supply destroyed by white hunters along the Missouri river and the fear of death by the fierce Sioux Indians in the buffalo country if they ventured to secure food in western Nebraska, they were reduced to a condition of slow starvation. They were hungry all the time.

The expedition, that overtook those miserable
Pawnee Indians and engaged them in the historic
though bloodless battle that gave to the village now
occupying the site of the Indian village the name of
Battle Creek, found the Indians without guards, as
hostile or well fed warriors would have had. They
were living in miserable wigwams scattered among
the trees on the river bank. They were living in
unspeakable poverty and filth. No doubt if the
expense of that so called greatest of Indian expeditions had been spent for food for those miserable
beings it would have been more effective than the
war-like demonstration. The expedition with its
lack of discipline, and the amount of whiskey they
drank, could have easily been defeated had the
Indians been well fed hostiles instead of hungry, depraved mendicants who had given up all hope.

Nebraska has been advertised over Europe and
America as the abiding place of the Indian and buffalo. Royal and titled people from Europe were en-
tertained by our military officers with the approval
of our government, by big buffalo hunts when those
wild cattle were plentiful. To make a success of
the hunt the best hunters and plainsmen were engaged. King Edward of England, when Prince of
Wales and only 18 years of age, came over well
chaperoned, and hunted buffalo under guard of a
military escort. Many other titled persons and big
game hunters visited our plains during the seventies. Reporters for eastern papers prepared in-
numerable highly colored articles for publication,
always advertising the Indian and buffalo. Then
most of the hunters, trappers and scouts delighted
in telling highly inflated and colored stories to the

reporters, much of it untrue. Nebraska was so
well advertised that when Buffalo Bill started his
Wild West show and visited all the important cities
of the northern states and principal countries of
Europe, the preliminary work to introduce him had
been laid by the reporters, and he only had to finish
it. Buffalo Bill's old stage coach, the band of howling, shooting, painted, war-bonneted Indians chas-
ing the coach that had the four horse team on the
run, and guards returning the fire, made a great
impression. Then at the proper time came the
heroic rescuer, Buffalo Bill, with all manner of frontier auxiliaries, and with an intrepid band of scouts
and frontier men, and rescued the hard pressed
overland coach by tickling the legs of the redskins
with burning powder from blank cartridges.

Probably no place in the world may be found a
tract of richer farming land, a more favorable climate for so many kinds of grain and temperate
zone fruit, than a strip 100 miles wide on the east
side of Nebraska and a mile on the west side of
Iowa facing the Missouri river, the southern end of
South Dakota and northeastern corner of Kansas
and northwestern corner of Missouri. Southeastern
Nebraska is largely devoted to raising apples and
hardy fruit. Chemists estimate that each acre of
the loess hilly land of northeastern Nebraska con-
tains many thousand dollars worth of phosphates
and minerals necessary for successful farming operations. Yet Nebraska was advertised to the world
by its Indians, buffaloes, wild game, desperate men
and desert land.

Indians and buffaloes were plentiful but never
helped develop the country. They were obstacles

that had to be removed before the natural resources could be utilized. Evidence is shown by remains of dwelling places that the country had been occupied along the Missouri, Platte and Loup rivers for ages by prehistoric people. From a hundred miles west of the Missouri river to eastern Colorado was the hunting ground of many tribes of Indians. It was given over to buffalo, elk, deer and wild water fowl. Prairie chickens came a little in advance of the settlers. Sentimental people always criticised the so called wrongs done in taking the land from the Indians. It was an economic necessity because they would not develop the land. The slaughter of buffaloes during the seventies has been bitterly resented. The immense herds that occupied the vast tract of fine farming lands extending from Texas to Manitoba were killed for sport or for their hides, even for the tongue or a choice sirloin or hump piece. Market hunters sent buffalo carcasses to market. It was a waste of wild buffalo but no other way was possible for improving the fine farming land and filling it with prosperous homes and beautiful towns and villages. The Indian had to go, or go to work. The buffalo had to go to make way for improved cattle that the white man produced. With the buffalo, went the Indians excepting those along the Missouri river who were willing to accept the white man's ways. The coyotes and rattlesnakes mostly followed the buffaloes and Indians.

During the early eighties the civilized Omaha Indians would go out into the state during the winter time to trap beaver and muskrats. They were not such nuisances as the Pawnees had been, yet they would visit farmers' homes and scare the women folks badly. They camped along the streams in the brush and readily ate the hogs that farmers had lost from cholera. In their flimsy, temporary tents they withstood a temperature of 15 below.

Indians and buffaloes are only incidental to Nebraska. The romance associated with them and the prominence they gave Nebraska only represented the mercenary offerings of newspaper propaganda and helped to attract people to wild west shows. The Indians who lived in the eastern part of Nebraska and activities of the first white people along the Missouri river tended to drive game away from a territory within 100 miles of the river.

The U. S. Bureau of Ethnology gives considerable information about Indian activities in Nebraska and near the Pawnee reservation agency, now the town of Genoa in Nance county. The Omaha Indians, either because they possessed a greater intelligence or because of contact with the early traders and missionaries, had always been prominent. Formerly they were warlike either from choice or necessity. The battle grounds between the Omahas and other Indians are given and four such conflicts are indicated in Boone county besides the one where Logan Fontanelle was killed. One adjoins Albion, the county seat, and is close to the remains of an Indian village. Two others are ten or more miles northwest in the little valley and another in the larger valley of the Cedar river.

One of the most favorably known Indians Nebraska ever produced was Logan Fontanelle, the son of a French trader, Lucian Fontanelle, and an Omaha Indian woman. The first traders appear to have been of French extraction and came up the river from the French colony at St. Louis. Lucian Fontanelle was reputed to have been a member of one of the royal families of France. His five children were given such education as was available and Logan later became chief of the Omahas and sought in many ways to elevate them. He was highly respected but called an Indian, although only a half breed.

Logan Fontanelle was killed in a conflict with the Sioux Indians while on a hunting trip with a part of the Omaha tribe in June, 1855. The place where he was killed has been claimed by different localities but the Bureau of Ethnology in a treatise on the Omaha Indians, definitely points to the place as on Beaver creek in Boone county northwest of Albion where the township line between 21 and 22 north crossed the creek. This was further verified by what a sister-in-law of Logan's told John Williamson, the former government farmer to instruct the Pawnees. He lived with them many years, went with them on their hunts and was with them when the great massacre by the Sioux at Ash Hollow encouraged them to move to the Indian territory. He went with them when they were moved and was sent by the government at different times to verify records with the Indians. On his last trip he talked with the old woman above mentioned and she described the place so minutely that Mr. Williamson thought he could locate it exactly.

It was the old story of the warlike Sioux interfering with other tribes in securing their supply of buffalo meat to which they had as much right as the Sioux.

Logan had headed a party of men, women and children and had gone to the buffalo range in what is now western Nebraska. They found the herds but as soon as they began the chase they were ambushed and driven away by the Sioux warriors. This interference was repeated till it was evident that to further attempt to kill buffalo would be useless and would invite massacre so they started on the return journey. They had seen no hostiles for several days and had camped at night near Beaver creek. As camp broke up next morning Logan and two other Indians started on ahead of the others. Logan rode down into a small ravine leading into the creek where he was picking gooseberries when he was surprised and before he could cross the creek and return to the others, was killed. The party was attacked and a battle continued till three o'clock in the afternoon when the Sioux withdrew. Several Omaha Indians were killed or wounded. The old woman told Mr. Williamson that they tied Logan's body on the back of a pony and took it back to Bellevue where he was buried.

Neither the Indian, buffalo, elk, deer or antelope, water fowl nor prairie chicken had anything to do with developing Nebraska. All except the migrating water fowl and prairie chickens had to go before the white man functioned successfully. There were no hostile Indians or buffaloes near Omaha after 1860. When the homesteaders first came prairie chickens were plentiful but soon there were a hundred hunters well equipped to kill game where there was one hunter during homestead days. A real hunter could go to the grass ranges 75 miles northwest of Boone county where occasionally a deer might be found, but they were few. Once a father and son, both experienced hunters, went up to the game country with the first snow hoping to secure a deer. They located deer at night and sought shelter in a homesteaders dugout where they slept on the floor. They arose before the family did and went out into the damp chilly snow without breakfast, and finally became exhausted and died from exposure.

One reason the homesteaders did not hunt prairie chickens much was because they were not able to finance a gun. Few had money to waste on ammunition. Few of them had even old army muskets yet the birds were plentiful. Their early morning drumming and cooing at their gathering grounds was interesting. A man equipped with a good gun, and only a town dweller would have a good gun, was known to have killed thirty or forty grown or nearly grown chickens during a two hour absence from home, and without the help of a dog.

In explanation of this, Fitz Sackett, who bought live stock and grain in company with Tom Riley of Albion, was an excellent shot and was equipped with an up-to-date breech loading, double-barreled shotgun. No one could get more chickens than Fitz could and he was a dead shot. Tom was a confirmed practical joker and never hesitated to play a joke on Fitz. He did it guardedly, mindful of after results. One day Tom carefully drew the shot from all of Fitz's shells and substituted salt for the shot and then induced Fitz to go out and get some prairie chickens. Fitz was hep and soon covies of chickens began to rise and Fitz worked the shotgun on them. He passed the first misses but when

misses followed with such regularity, he wondered.
When they continued his suspicion was aroused and
he started to examine the shells. Tom realized that
the proper time for his departure had arrived and
started on a fast run for home. That told the story
to Fitz and he began pumping salt after the fast
vanishing Tom as rapidly as the gun would function.

I had brought from Indiana an ancient Austrian
musket that someone had turned into a single barrel,
muzzle loading shotgun.   At rare periods I went
gunning for chickens.   Once I flushed a covey of
nearly grown chickens and as they took the air
about 100 feet away I killed three chickens with
that one shot.

We lived on our farm on a hill with a magnificent
view of Beaver valley.   Our sod house was about
forty rods away at the bottom of the hill with the
stable near it. We used water from the dug well
by the sod house, not yet having made the well by
our new frame house.   My brother-in-law who
came from Indiana with us, was always for business
and had no intention of wasting time hunting. But
he had brought one of the made over Mexican war
army muskets that in the beginning of the Civil war
were used till better arms could be provided. They
were loaded with a big ball and three buckshot and
were purposely made to kick hard so that in volley
firing the fact of the discharge might be known and
the danger of putting a second load on top of the
first one avoided.   They made quite good muzzle
load shotguns charged with bird shot, but were un-
merciful kickers.

One day something occurred to interfere with
farm work and he loaded the musket and took

our five year old boy with him and started in the
lumber wagon drawn by the farm team, for a
chicken hunt. From our hill my wife could see the
team and the boy at a distance of a third of a mile
on the prairie with the boy sitting down close to
the dash board holding the lines. She saw her
brother stand up in the back end of the wagon and
aim at something in the grass. He took no chances
on a wing shot. Then the roar of the gun came
and the rebound kicked him out of the wagon and
the horses ran away with the boy holding the lines.
Of course they started for their stable at home. A
grove of trees obscured the view but the mother
was frantic with fear for the safety of her boy. She
met them at the stable yard and caught the outside
rein of one, but around and around the hay stack
they went, against the pig yard and then over the
side of the dug well with a near approach to the
boy falling into it. Finally they stopped and her
brother, who was not hurt, arrived and everything
was made safe.

When I came home from my office it was plain
that they had all been given a nervous shock. The
boy had gone to sleep and when I reprimanded him
for running my horses he rose to the occasion and
explained that he had tried as hard as he could to
check them. Brother-in-law brought the old musket
and gave it to me and said, "Here is my gun. I am
not going to hunt any more." It was a doubtful
gift and while he was known to accompany someone for a short hunt for chickens, ducks or rabbits,
to carry the game, he hunted no more.

Later pot hunters decimated the chickens for the
market and finally chickens became as scarce as the

Indians and buffaloes and began to follow the going
of all wild things to make way for civilization.
Homesteaders never cared to hunt and even the
small outlay in cash for ammunition was more than
they could afford. Most of their purchases had to
be paid for in work. What they could not work
for they had to go without. They could not trade
work for powder and shot. They exchanged work
with their neighbors and bought things they could
trade work for.

Nearly all over the grain producing section of
Nebraska the first towns were located by a water
power. Three were so located in Boone county. It
was the paramount wish of first settlers that they
secure a flouring mill and a newspaper. They would
vote bonds to help a mill or subscribe donations to
help a mill or newspaper to operate among them.
As illustrative of the way things were accomplished
without money, in 1876, Fitz Sackett and William
Crouch, two young Wisconsin men, who had a limited knowledge of milling, secured the Beaver Creek
mill site near Albion and began the erection of a
water mill and a dam across the creek with a dug
race to convey the water to the mill. It took lots
of team work to dig the race, make the dam and
haul lumber from Columbus fifty miles away. The
promoters had no money but hired the settlers to
help make the mill and wait for their pay till the
mill was in operation. The settlers agreed to the
proposition because they could not find work for
money anywhere. Fitz was the one who did the
talking to hypnotize the settlers but one day one of
them demanded money. Fitz explained that they
had no money and the agreement which they ex-

pected to comply with to pay money as soon as they got the mill into earning. The man was obstinate and gave notice that he must have money or there would be a fight, and he would take it out of the mill promoter's hide. The way for payment looked open to Fitz and his easiest way to pay what they owed, so he shed his coat and started out in the open and proclaimed to the workmen, "Come on, you dirty whelps, and get your pay."

The mill was finally finished and operated successfully and beneficially for the settlers for years. First, Crouch dropped out of the company and then Fitz sold the mill and half section of land for a song and traded his large stock of farm implements for a flock of sheep. He did not know that the sheep had been brought in from Texas and were diseased with scab and he lost most of them. Milling was finally abandoned by the antiquated burr mill and a more modern roller mill was built on the side track up town and operated for years. The water power plant was later used to generate electric energy by the local power and light company.

Burning of the prairie grass in late fall or early spring influenced the movements of buffalo, elk, deer and antelope. It also caused the death of many prairie chickens and quail and deprived them of the good sheltered places they had been accustomed to occupy. A prairie fire going before a head wind blowing a gale from the northwest was a fearsome thing. Homesteaders protected their farms, hay stacks and buildings by plowing fire guards and by burning the grass on wide strips around their premises but where no impediments of this sort were encountered the fire went at a speed of a running horse, slowing somewhat in the short grass of the high land. Anything alive in front of that fire was in great danger and much loss of life resulted among live stock and tame things when the fire broke loose. The approach of a prairie fire to a town always brought out the able bodied men to guard against the danger.

CHAPTER VII

Grasshoppers—Drouth
Colonization

"Breathes there the man with soul so dead
Who never to himself has said:
    This is my own, my native land?"

—*Scott*

THE grasshopper visitations to Nebraska and Kansas during the seventies, especially to Nebraska, gave a great deal of damaging advertising. The opinion that eastern people formed from the exaggerated reports sent to the newspapers was that the grasshoppers just came down like a wide spread rain and hail and covered a large area at once. They were led to believe that this big grasshopper shower fell in 1876 and that they ate up everything. The truth is that they had been coming in small swarms for years and had at times damaged the few crops the settlers had. With a fully developed country their visitation would not have been noticed much. After 1876 they came along year by year for some time, but did no damage. I was told by my renter that a large swarm in passing in 1879 were caused to light on our wheat field because of adverse winds. He thought the wheat would be destroyed but the wind abated and they rose and passed on without doing damage. I saw them passing over in 1881 and they were seen even later. The ones I saw were flying high in the air and could be seen by the silvery glistening of their wings caused by the reflection of the sun. They did not stop, and like the wind no one knew from whence they came or whither they were going.

It must not be presumed that the swarms came down and covered a wide area evenly. The air might be dark with them for a considerable space and when compelled by wind, or other reason to mankind unknown, they came down and where they stopped they were very thick. It has been claimed by railroad men that they interfered with the passage of railroad trains. Settlers suffered greatly from them but they had small crops to lose.

Rev. C. W. Wells in his book, "Frontier Life," mentions that the seasons were dry and crops light in 1875 and 1876. He says that in some places the grasshoppers were very thick. They came down in bunches. He has this to say about these particular years:

"This year we had another very dry season resulting in light crops on which the grasshoppers came down by multiplied millions. Great destitution and suffering followed and it was hard for the preacher to obtain support. The grasshoppers came in such swarms that they looked in the distance like fast-gathering rain clouds flying through the air. In some places on the fields of grain they were so numerous that the grain was completely hid from sight. If they had kept still, a man with a scoop shovel could have filled a common wagon bed with them in a few minutes. For a number of years it seemed to be our lot to meet with the grasshoppers, which would take meat, bread and other things from our table."

J. W. Turner, an Englishman who came directly from city life in England to take a homestead in Nebraska, at a later date published his experiences in a book, "Pioneers of the West," stated that the grasshoppers came in relays extending over quite a length of time. He tried to smoke them away from his wheat field but it had little effect. Still they left him a fair crop of wheat. After the wheat crop was harvested another swarm stopped and ate up his sod corn, beans and garden vegetables, except some potatoes. He saved from his ten acres of wheat and garden, 120 bushels of wheat and 15 bushels of potatoes. He said a trial to endure was the ridicule of some of the people in the eastern states but others came nobly to their relief and sent them clothing and food. Mr. Turner said that it was hard to exaggerate about them. I quote from his book:

"They drifted over in such clouds as to blacken the whole heavens, and with such a buzzing, roaring noise that it could be heard a long time before they came over us. Sometimes they would fly low, and at other times they would be far above us, drifting along by the myriads, their gauzy wings glistening like tiny bits of silver. And as they would gently fall to the earth, like a sky lark with out-stretched wings falling out of the heavens, the sight was much like that of large snow flakes in a gentle storm. When they settled down the corn and vegetables would be so completely covered as to be black with them one over another. The corn was their first choice. When they had stripped it of every particle of foliage—which they would in a night—they would stick so thick on the stumps of stalks that there would be no room to stick the point of a finger. They would be so thick that the ground could not be seen. They would swarm in the roads and be crushed under the wheels of a wagon, and we would be obliged to tie our pants around the bottom with a string to keep them from trespassing. For the sensation was just about as pleasant as the crawling of a snake would be with a gentle waking up of their finely adjusted forceps into the bargain. As we walked along they would rise from the ground in such clouds and swarms that we had to fight our way through them. It was a time when nobody needed to be admonished to keep his mouth shut."

So here is the evidence of two eye witnesses. Instead of one or two years the grasshoppers had been passing by about ten years. Perhaps dry years assisted in hatching out swarms where they had made stops and finally unfavorable seasons exterminated them. They were not well understood and there is no record of a previous or later visitation. They may have developed by the great drouth that visited the middle west from the Alleghany to the Rocky mountains during the early seventies. It was in 1871 that so many disastrous fires occurred in the pineries of Michigan and other northern states. In the lake region small patches of timber that had been left in swampy places burned, even the earth burned down to the clay subsoil and let the trees fall by the removal of supporting roots and moss. It was the year that the great Chicago fire took such heavy toll. Many lives were lost in the Chicago fire, the lumber camps and settlements in the timber of Michigan, Wisconsin and Minnesota. Nebraska happened to get the grasshoppers that came as an aftermath.

The eighties saw Nebraska prospering and making progress. Then the moderately dry years of 1892 and 1893 with the financial panic of 1893, left a mark on Nebraska, and it cut deep. The only complete crop failure eastern Nebraska ever experienced was in 1894. But what seemed then to be a great calamity, in the end proved a lasting benefit. All manner of scrub stock of horses, cattle and hogs had been brought to the state by the settlers. It all had to go because scarcely a bit of stock forage remained after the lack of rain and the hot winds that came up from Kansas about the middle of July in 1894. Corn under cultivation had grown pretty well and was tasseled out but the hot wind killed the tassels and left all the leaves and stalks as white as though they had been lapped by a blaze. Rains soon came and in abundance but the crop was gone. All the cattle and poor horses were disposed of. Young pigs were killed and larger ones shipped out. I was keeping two cows for milk supply for our family. I sold them to the butcher for a cent and a quarter a pound and it was the butcher's boast that he sold them back to me for table use for fifteen cents a pound.

But the weeds that had begun to hurt crops on cultivated land were killed and the farmers started with clean fields and the stock they brought in was of a superior, pure bred class. Grain crops were large but the aftermath of the 1893 financial panic kept prices down. The immense fields of corn yielded wonderfully, and as there were no cattle and hogs to fatten, it had to be sold to ship away. Farmers sold their corn, both shelled and in the ear, for nine to eleven cents a bushel.

The remarkable sandhill country claimed a small corner of Boone county. It was little known and some of it was not explored till about 1880. What I noticed was that in a grain country like Boone it was an advantage to have cheap pasture land so nearby. We could send our stock cattle to the sand-hills and have them herded for a dollar each for the entire season while we were raising corn to fat-ten them in the fall of the year. The sandhills, as I knew them prior to the 1894 drouth, had many small ponds or lakes scattered between the hills. They never went dry and even a pond covering an acre of ground was well stocked with sun fish, bull heads or croppies. Since the 1894 drouth, when those ponds dried up, no fish have been found in them except in the larger ones fed by underflow springs. It seemed good proof that the drouth of the early nineties was the first one of its kind that the country could have passed through, at least for many years past. Otherwise, how could the fish have been found in the ponds.

The Nebraska sandhill country has never been fully understood. It is destined to become very valuable. It is not a widely uniformly sand covered section of the state like a sandy desert. The sandhills of shifting sand are in limited areas. Large tracts of bottom land between hills were covered by heavy growths of grass that make valuable hay land. Naturally it is covered by blue stem wild grass while the high lands have a short growth of gramma. Cattle wintered on the short grass, reach market as fat as corn fed stock from the grain sections. Timothy or red top tame grass sown on the wild hay meadows soon crowded out the wild grass. Large tracts of rich sandy land or clay spots among the sandhills afford a great deal of good farming land. The whole sandhill country would support forest trees, and the spaces between the hills are suitable for fruit if protected from fire.

Sandy land endures drouth better than the heavy loess soil. Most of the corn raised in the grain sections of Nebraska in 1894 was grown on sandy land. Much of the sandhill country may be made available for diversified crops if properly handled to keep the top from shifting. Such farms have been reclaimed by sowing rye and plowing it under or by covering with coarse litter from feed lots or farm stables.

During the period that the eastern half of Nebraska was being transferred from a homeless prairie into a grain producing country with growing towns and improved farm homes, the western part that had been the favorite grazing land for vast herds of buffalo, deer and antelope, and their accompanying scavengers, coyotes, wolves, and Indians, was being transferred into a grazing land for domestic, or half wild broad horn cattle from Texas. Beginning shortly after the close of the Civil war, enterprising cattle men began to gather herds of half wild Texas cattle and drive them north to a shipping point and soon the drives carried great herds of cattle into western Nebraska. As time passed the quality of those cattle was improved by the introduction of high grade domestic stock among them. So while the grain sections of he state were being placed under culivation, the western part was being stocked with great herds of cattle that had long ranges where no farming had been attempted.

Concentration points for the cattle during he summer and sheltering and feeding places during the winter when the snow might cover the nourishing gramma or buffalo grass, were called ranches. Each ranch man had his brand with which he marked his cattle. The branding iron at the end of an iron rod about four feet long and the brand mark might be anything the owner designed. If his brand was registered he would be protected in its use. When a ranchman bought cattle they were promptly branded. The cattle were permitted to run at large during the summer and in the fall a "round up" was held in which representatives from all ranches participated and sorted and branded their own stock and drove them to the home ranch. The calves went with their branded mothers but unbranded calves, called "mavericks" were divided among the cattle men and branded in obedience to a law of their own.

Branding was done by concentrating the cattle at a convenient place where a fire was built of wood brought for the purpose. The iron would be kept in the fire where it would remain red hot. The cowboys on their trained ponies ran the half wild cattle down and threw their lassos, a long rope with a running noose at one end and the other tied to the horn of the saddle, and caught the sought animal around the horns, if possible, and started with him towards the branding fire. If he hesitated another cowboy roped his hind legs and the unfortunate animal was dragged by his feet or head or any way, hurriedly to the brander. The branding iron heated red was pressed firmly on the spot designated for the ranch brand, it might be right or left hip, flank or shoulder. Soon the smell of burning hair and flesh arose in the air accompanied by the bellowing of the animal, but the ordeal was short. Dishonest ranchmen sometimes placed their brand over a dim one of another ranch and claimed possession of the animal.

The common way of escorting a colony of emigrant cattle into the sandhill section of western Nebraska was to gather in Texas two or three thousand head of different sizes and ages and drive them slowly north. Eight or ten cowboys under a foreman was required to drive the cattle. A "chuck wagon," as the provision wagon was called, carried the food supplies and the bed rolls of the herders. The cook was always with the chuck wagon. A horse wrangler took charge of the riding ponies of which each herder must have several, and the herders went on duty as herdsmen in relays to watch the cattle at night. The men all slept on the ground. The cattle were driven slowly along and grazed as they went. But few miles a day could be covered and it took months to deliver them in the sandhills of Nebraska.

At night the cattle would be bedded down or encouraged to lie quietly together much as wild buffalo were accustomed to. Sometimes something frightened them and they stampeded and that always meant sleepless days and nights of the hardest kind of labor to gather them again. Then Indians had to be reckoned with for some years. At day break the cattle began to move and seek pasturage and the wrangler would bring in the horses and wake up the men. The cook had been awakened earlier and had prepared breakfast and the cattle were slowly drifted in the direction designed to take.

When rivers were reached they had to be forded, no matter if in flood stage. The cattle were urged into the stream and cowboys rode on each side, swimming their horses where necessary, and never a chance to dry their clothes except by the sun and wind. Sometimes the cattle refused to cross rivers in a body and a stampede was on and the cattle scattered and it would take days to get them together again. In the meantime the cowboys went sleepless and there never was a moment when their clothes were dry. As a rule they remained healthy but the strenuous work encouraged them to dissipation when their work on the trip was finished. On the ranches the work was something the same and a hard life during the summer putting up hay, watching stock and at the roundups roping and branding cattle. In the winter those who remained around the ranch worked for their board or for small wages.

The sandhill country was the objective of many of those big herds and for some time ranches were at least twenty miles apart and each ranch kept

thousands of cattle. Mayor James Dahlman of
Omaha graphically described in a paper he read before a meeting of the Nebraska Historical Society
the hardships of herding cattle in the sandhills. He
grew up a cowboy in the Texas cattle country.
March, 1878, found him a cow puncher on a sandhill ranch. He described the sandhills and an experience he had soon after his arrival at the ranch.

"The section of country north and west of Niobrara, was used as winter and summer range up to
1878. South and east of the river was known as the
sandhill desert, and was considered unsafe for man
or beast to roam in. Line riders were stationed
along the edge of the sandhills to keep cattle from
drifting into the hills during the storms. In March,
1878, a terrific snow storm drove cattle through the
lines. Our ranch had over 6,000 cattle in this predicament and it was feared they were lost because
the section they went to was unknown. In April
the foreman selected twelve men and selected saddle
ponies, took a cook wagon and invaded the desert,
as it was called, to try and retrieve cattle. They
started April 15 and the second day out met a
frightful snowy blizzard that lasted three days. It
was difficult to keep warm and all the fuel they could
get was the wood brought in the chuck wagon for
cooking purposes and cow and buffalo chips. The
storm over, they started out and soon began to
strike cattle that were perfectly contented and fat
as though grain fed. With plenty of water and good
pasturage on the short dry buffalo grass that is very
nourishing in the winter, they had come through
rolling in fat. Unbranded cattle from one to four

years old were as fat as though they had come out
of feed lots where they had been corn fed."

Mr. Dahlman tells how he and his partner noticed
a fourteen hundred pound cow just rolling in fat and
proposed to rope and tie her and bring up the cook
wagon and have some prime beef to add to their
ration of poor bacon. He roped the cow's horns the
first throw but she was so big and strong and going
so fast that she threw the pony, rider and all and
with the rope tied to the saddle horn was going on
her way with them when the other man roped her
legs. They soon hog tied her and the camp ration
was helped by the addition of prime beef. He said
they gathered 8,000 head of their own cattle and
300 mavericks or unbranded cattle, that by the rules
of the range, went to the ranch they worked for.

Around those ranches, or at nearby rail points
when the railroads came in, villages were started.
They were colonized by accretion as most colonies of
the state were. A notable example of organized
colonization where advance scouts searched out a
suitable location for a whole neighborhood of people
living in the older parts of the country, was the
locating of a Wisconsin colony on land that later became the city of Norfolk, Nebraska. As the buffalo
were supplanted by colonies of domestic cattle in the
pasturage sections of Nebraska, so did the Wisconsin colony of men, women and children supplant
Indians and possess the grain section of northeastern Nebraska and build their homes close together
with their improved farms, and establish schools,
churches and an orderly system of government.

Norfolk, the leading railroad center of northeastern Nebraska, was occupied by an organized colony

of 125 men, women and children who came from Wisconsin with their household goods in wagons and driving their livestock with them.

The marauding Pawnee Indians had been quieted in northeastern Nebraska in 1859 but settlers were still fearful and no settlements had been made beyond West Point. It was an unoccupied country that Herman Braasch and Frederick Wagner, acting as scouts for a German community in Jefferson county, Wisconsin, visited in northeastern Nebraska. They had left Wisconsin September 1, 1865, and traveled by way of St. Joseph, Missouri, Omaha, Elkhorn City, Fontanelle and West Point, Nebraska. The advance settler was found eight miles beyond West Point. At West Point they hired a man and team to take them on an inspection tour farther up the valley and away from settlements. About four miles above the confluence of the north fork of the Elkhorn river with the main stream, they decided as a suitable site for the colony they proposed to return with to occupy. They then concluded their search for a location that would accommodate their people and returned to Wisconsin to report. Arriving at home before winter they found their neighbors agreeable to accept their report and the time till spring was employed in preparing for the long emigration journey that they must take.

May 14, 1866, the colony started their long journey with 24 families consisting of about 125 people in covered wagons driving their cattle with them, prepared to occupy the land their scouts had approved. After enduring hardships, not the least being bad roads or no roads at all, they finally arrived at the limit of civilization at West Point in Cuming county, July 4, 1866. It took them till July 17 to reach the place where they proposed to settle, but the journey from West Point compelled them to make crossings and rude bridges across a number of streams. On arriving at their destination they found the spot that had been selected was already occupied by a small party of young men from Illinois. The Illinois party had arrived in May and squatted on the land. One of them, Matthias Kerr, had taken possession of a tract of land that fronted the river but extended back from the river some distance. He had broken a small tract of prairie. A council was held and the Illinois party realizing that intermingling with such a large party of German speaking people, who had lived as neighbors and belonged to the same Lutheran church, would not be agreeable for either party as they themselves were all English speaking people having other church affiliation. A mutual agreement was reached whereby the Illinois men, for a small consideration, agreed to locate elsewhere. Mr. Kerr having made the greatest improvements received $200 and the party went to the present site of Madison, later the county seat of Madison county, and made a new location. The county was named by act of the territorial legislature.

Probably this German colony was the only complete colony that came in a body to locate in northern Nebraska. Their former acquaintance permitted them to keep together and retain their former habits and church relations. Their history and their journey to the new land and their successful home making was a romantic one that would make an easy foundation on which to build a book. Nebraska was reclaimed by the typical Nebraskan, the fruit of the melting pot, into which so many nationalities and many states furnished representatives, all bringing the characteristics of their nationalities and habits of the place of their birth with them. Hundreds of colonies worked for the development of Nebraska but they were mostly colonies by accretion. A family from a certain state would locate in the new country and his neighbors would begin to join him to be near acquaintances or fellow countrymen, but the Norfolk colony was a real, premeditated colony, planned and carried out in a body.

So this colony located on the land their scouts had chosen. The name "North Fork" was finally changed to "Norfolk," a name that the prosperous railroad city was later to carry.

At first the colonist families lived in their covered wagons, but they lived and worked in harmony. Church services and preaching were observed from the first. Before making their houses, a satisfactory division and choice of land to be occupied by the different families had to be arranged. With a pocket compass and harness lines for surveyor's compass and chains, tracts were laid off to contain 160 acres each fronting narrowly on the river on each side and extending back far enough to encompass 160 acres of land. This gave each family access to the water of the river and close enough to each other for protection in case of trouble with Indians. After the land had been surveyed, a slip of paper carrying the number of one of the tracts of land was drawn from a hat by a blindfolded man and another paper bearing the name of a head of a family was drawn from another hat by another blindfolded man. The tract drawn was the allotment of the one whose name was written on the slip of paper. No complaints were made and everybody was satisfied.

The same co-operation and organization continued in building log houses for each family. Logs were available and were used to make the first houses, for the settlers had not yet learned the art of making sod houses. Before winter set in every family was comfortably housed. The first store opened in Norfolk or Madison county was established for the retail of goods to the colony in a dugout near the river bank close by what is now the main street of the city of Norfolk. A man named Jones was owner of this first store which began business in November, 1866.

As a mill site was usually the inducement for the first settler to locate nearby, so did the scouts discover that an excellent mill site was found by the land they selected for the settlers homes. A flourishing mill was established there and in operation in 1870 and never ceased to function after its establishment.

A Lutheran Parochial School and regular church services had been established and continued from the time of the first meeting held around a covered wagon. A year after the arrival of the colony, Herman Braasch, the man who led the colony to this land of Canaan, bought logs enough a few miles away for $40 to make a log church and in it the colony held church services till the year 1878 when the log church was replaced by a neat frame building.

The colonists always lived harmoniously together and their descendants continued to carry on, but like all others who were cast in the molds to make Nebraska citizens, they were affected somewhat by changes, some leaving and others joining them. Theirs was an interesting community experience that demonstrated the value of co-operation while the usual typical Nebraskans experience was individual.

CHAPTER VIII

The Nebraska Climate

"Announced by all the trumpets of the sky,
Arrives the snow, and, driving o'er the fields
Seem nowhere to alight; the whited air
Hides hills and woods, the river and the heaven,
And veils the farm house at the garden's end."
—*Emerson.*

THE climate of no state has been so unjustly slandered as has that of Nebraska. Compared with Florida, there is a greater variation between the summers and winters of Nebraska but there is less variation between noon and midnight. Nebraska has glorious falls and usually fine summer weather. Open or warm winters in the same latitude in the lake regions are periods to be dreaded because of the moist atmosphere and mud. It is not so in Nebraska. I have known farmers in eastern Nebraska to plow every month of the year, and March, usually a dismal month in other states, is commonly a favorable month for seeding the land to spring grain, or plowing for corn. Homesteaders who sowed spring wheat on the last year sod breaking, usually sowed in February and while the wheat did not germinate till later, it had such an early start that it matured before the warm July sun hurried it so that the grains were shrunken or did not appear at all. Sometimes when farmers grew winter wheat it would be sown so late in the fall that it did not germinate at all till the next April yet produced a good crop at harvest time.

But winters were not invariably warm and open. As a rule, the Indian summer weather held well into early winter, and January and February alternated between snow storms and mild dry weather. I was a general practitioner of medicine during the winter of 1881 and 1882 and was out of doors a great deal. One little cold period in November the temperature went to seven below. It never reached zero weather again that winter. Homesteaders and settlers on the uplands between valleys, lived in dugouts and sod houses and lacked means to buy necessary clothing. The night would be clear and star lighted with frost on the ground in the morning yet the days were warm and sunshiny and dry and the weather lovely. 1 have seen settlers' children running around out doors barefoot in February, apparently without discomfort.

California and Florida are hopelessly outclassed by Nebraska fall weather and sometimes Nebraska winters are equally pleasant. If the winters could be condensed into January and February, Nebraska climate would be above reproach. A short period of winter is not unpleasant and is healthy. April is really Nebraska's most unpleasant month of the year with cold winds that cease when spring rains begin to fall. The dry cold of twenty below is not felt as much as a damp, chilly cold of ten below in the great lake territory. Exposure to 25 below, no matter how hard it was snowing, seldom took a Nebraska settler's life. It was the 25 to 35 above temperature with a wet snow driven by a hard wind that caused loss of life when exposure was long continued.

Early day stories about the cold Nebraska climate turned many people away who would have prospered and made good citizens. Those stories have never been forgotten. Even as late as 1923 while spending a season in New Orleans, my admission that I lived in Nebraska brought shudders and sympathy about the cold Nebraska climate. At the same time Nebraska was enjoying finer sunshiny weather, much less chilly than the New Orleans climate dripping with chilly rain. Even in March on my way north when I stopped over a day at Vicksburg, Mississippi, to visit the Civil war battlefields, it was snowing and I never suffered more from cold than I did from the chilly air that day.

People contemplating going to Nebraska to homestead land were confronted with the dismal stories of blizzards, tornadoes, hot winds, cold winds, dry winds, just winds, Indians, rattlesnakes, grasshoppers, lack of rain and many other things bad and nothing good. Experience has proven that the conditions and climate were much the same as in the latitude of the great lakes directly eastward except that open winters were dry and pleasant in Nebraska, and wet, muddy and disagreeable in the lake regions. Cyclones that brought destruction at infrequent periods, visited southeastern Nebraska but they also visited the region of the great lakes. Rainfall did not change much as shown by records kept from the early fifties. Cultivation of the soil permitted the rain water to enter the ground instead of hurriedly running off into streams to cause great floods. There was never a visitation of grasshoppers after the seventies and with the country fully cropped, the damage they did in 1876 when the crops

Discouraged. Ejected From the Homestead: Going Back East to Old Home.

Genuine Sioux Indian Pony, Carrying White Children.

were meager, would hardly be duplicated again.

The blizzards that gave Nebraska such a bleak name are exactly such as I have been out in many times in northern Indiana. One exposed to the chilly, damp snow, especially when he has been long without food, might be in danger of being chilled to death. So people have lost their lives in every state in the union. Even states bordering on the Gulf of Mexico are not immune from such dangers. Probably the worst storm of this class that ever visited Nebraska, came in April 1873, when the country not bordering on the Missouri river, was sparsely settled. It lasted three days and came following a warm rain that turned to a wet snow and filled ravines and hollows and caused some loss of live stock.

A prosperous Nebraskan who passed through that storm told me that he had filed on his homestead claim in March and built a small sod house about 12x16 feet in size. As he was a single man without a family it was large enough for one lone bachelor. He owned a yoke of oxen but no other live stock. Not expecting such a visitor as the blizzard, he had not been to get his bread that a woman living two miles away baked for him, and his cupboard was as bare as Mother Hubbard's cupboard. The storm came on and shut him in at home. The ground being level, prevented snow from drifting around his sod house. His bed tick was filled with buckwheat straw and he had a little buckwheat bran in his hut. To save his oxen he brought them into the house and sustained them on the buckwheat straw from his bed. The buckwheat bran he used to make griddle cakes for himself. Buckwheat bran and buckwheat straw was not likely to overnourish man or beast. The storm left him discouraged and he returned to eastern Nebraska intending to abandon such a frightful climate, but good advice sent him back. He died years after possessed of much good land and other property and never saw another storm as bad as the one of April, 1873.

A blizzard that gave Nebraska a great deal of adverse advertising came January 12, 1888. The forenoon had been warm with a south wind and a light mist falling. About midday a cold wave came up from the northwest so suddenly that many people did not notice its approach till it was on them. The temperature during the afternoon was around forty above. The storm originated somewhere in the northwest and extended to the Missouri and Platte rivers. The country was pretty well settled but landmarks of trees, fences and large buildings had not yet been established. The unbroken prairie was covered with dry grass. Soon the grass was filled with snow and in the absence of trees and fence, a person out in the storm could detect no difference between looking into flying snow and the snow on the ground. There was said to have been some loss of life on the cattle ranges in western Nebraska. Many people who had gone from home lightly clad suffered from the chilly air and some were frost bitten. Eastern Nebraska in the farming sections had no loss of life.

Hundreds of country schools were in session and the warm forenoon had brought a good attendance. Those children were all taken home in safety, although they might live several miles from the school house. The procedure was that in some instances farmers came with horse teams before the storm had been raging long and got their children and took others going the same directions with them to their homes. In other instances the teacher sent the largest boys to lead the procession and break a path through the snow and she acted as file closer to keep the small children in the path till their homes were reached or left them in a neighbor's house where they stayed all night.

The blizzard attracted the daily papers and their reporters got busy with news scoops. There were many attractive young women teaching country schools. They were red blooded and filled with the joy of vigorous life. Naturally the young men who reported the storm to their papers made heroines of the teachers, and many colorful stories filled the daily papers throughout the country showing the courage and resourcefulness of the teachers in saving their pupils from death in the alleged awful storm. The stories clung, and the free adverse advertising did Nebraska great injustice and harm.

Among the hundreds of teachers who were caught with their pupils in the country school houses when the storm came up was Miss Minnie Freeman. She was teaching in one of the sparsely settled country school districts northwest of Grand Island. A versatile reporter heard of her experience and flooded the papers with her heroism. She was a bright, capable young woman and later became the wife of a prosperous business man and was herself a leader in woman's club activities. She did all she could and conducted the retreat wisely, but her experience was only like many other teachers shared, all of whom demonstrated their ability to act when suddenly thrown on their own responsibility.

Miss Freeman, realizing that a bad storm was on and that the children should be sent home, dismissed school and started the line of retreat with the largest boys ahead and she brought up the rear with the smaller children till all were safely housed at a neighbors or taken to their homes. There was little danger, little suffering but a competent young Nebraska woman acted wisely and quickly. Yet the colorful report, greatly amplified, may be heard in distant places today. Twenty years after the storm I visited St. Petersburg, Florida, and heard the Minnie Freeman story with all the horrors of an Arctic storm accompaniment being discussed among those at the table where I ate my first meal in that town.

Holt county was the western line of settlers and families at the time of the 1888 storm and beyond was a cattle range country. There were possibly deaths from exposure along the 300 mile range section from losing the way on the bare prairies. Holt county had country schools and in one of them Miss Eleanor C. Brown was the teacher. She managed her flock of scholars wiser than Miss Freeman did and showed good judgment in keeping them in the school house till next morning. As usual with frontier school houses, it was located some distance from any of the scholars' homes. This school house was a small frame wooden building on the open prairie, with no vestibule and door opening directly outside. It was warmed by a small upright stove. The storm came up and it was apparent to the teacher that it would be impossible to deliver the children at their scattered homes without help. Fortunately there was a supply of coal on the ground outside the school house. A quantity of this coal was carried in by the largest boys. The small children had to be amused to keep them from becoming frightened. The teacher saved her own lunch to give the children during the night when they would become hungry. A rousing fire was kept up all night and by the ruddy glow of the stove, games were played and other means taken to divert the attention of the children from their predicament.

Morning came and with it one of the men who had children at school, arrived with a sled and horse team and helped the teacher convey the children to their homes or to a neighboring house where they would be safe. The man who rescued them had made the attempt the night before but had missed the school house and brought up at the town of Inman three miles away. He remained till next morning and about 10 a. m. arrived at the school house. The teacher reached her boarding place where she found the housewife alone with her children. The woman was in feeble health and the children were young and not strong. It was necessary to go to the relief of the family cow that was snow bound in her stable a short distance from the house. Miss Brown at once joined the children and shoveled snow nearly all the rest of the day to liberate the cow. The local color given to the stories sent out by newspaper reporters to daily papers about a snow storm, that would cause no more comment twenty years later than it would in the middle west states, was injurious to Nebraska. Those re-

porters gave Nebraska a climate that would put
Alaska to shame.

The case of Willie Saxton was given wide publicity. He was an 18 year old boy living with his
father on the cattle ranges in the northwestern corner of Boone county. The morning of the blizzard
being warm, Willie left home thinly clad to go some
distance across the unfenced prairie with a team of
horses to get a load of hay. He was caught in the
storm and soon became bewildered and lost and before he reached home his hands and feet were badly
frozen. The county superintendent of schools, a
young man lately from an eastern college, interested
himself in the boy and led a movement to help him
to an education. Much publicity was given the
Willie Saxton case.

The C. & N. W. railroad section boss at Bradish
in the eastern side of Boone county, had tied his
cow out with a long rope where she could get fresh
air and graze on the wild grass. After he came in
off the section he went to retrieve her and bring her
to her stable. As he had taken her some distance
from the section house he became lost and took
shelter in an abandoned sod house that was without
windows or door to close the openings. Like others
who were frosted in the storm he was insufficiently
clothed and before morning he was so badly frost
bitten that he had to go to a hospital for treatment.

CHAPTER IX

Pioneer District Schools

"The school boy, with his satchel in his hand,
Whistling aloud to bear his courage up,
And lightly tripping o'er the long flat stones."
—*Blair.*

THE common school system established by early Nebraska settlers was the keystone of progress and mental development of the state. This assertion admits of no controversy. It was the cornerstone of the Nebraska temple, and the poor settlers, most of them having had limited school opportunities, planned from the first to give their children all the education they possibly could so that they would not go forth to fight their world battles handicapped as they had themselves gone. It was the exception that a settler planned to leave his children land and money instead of education. The management of country school affairs is based upon the town meeting system of early New England and is far closer to a rule of the people, by the people and for the people than the modern administration fallacies put into effect by politicians, who have axes to grind. From the little sod school house to the model country school houses that later became so numerous in Nebraska, the country schools have been the greatest uplift that Nebraska has had. They were the feeders for the town high schools, and they in turn for the normals, junior colleges and state university.

With the early district schools were the young women teachers. They were physically and mentally strong, fearless and defiant of obstacles, determined that they would establish a reputation for all things good and be an example to direct the young people to higher life, they left their mark on Nebraska citizenship that can never be effaced. The most of them married and established homes that were models of domestic efficiency and became model housekeepers as they had been models as teachers. Many of those teachers homesteaded land themselves. The homestead law required a married settler to reside continuously on his claim, but a single person was allowed to occupy the claim intermittingly, it being recognized that a chance must be given to be off the land at times to earn part of their support. No young woman who would go out to a small shanty or sod house and stay alone nights, far from neighbors, with coyotes howling nearby, could lack resolution. I have seen small sod houses, far from neighbors that a teacher occupied and stayed alone nights enough to make final proof to the land.

Many of the pioneer teachers taught in small log or frame houses so open that the sun could enter through the crevices. Added to the insufficient fuel supply the sod school houses were far more comfortable than the frame or log buildings. The boarding places of the teachers, were of a necessity, often a mile or more away from the school house and accommodations much like camping out. A former teacher explained that the school house she taught in was made of logs and was so open where the "chinks" had been left out between the logs that a fairly good view of the outdoor landscape was possible. Then with a limited supply of green cottonwood fuel, that the teacher must use to warm the school house in time for morning classes, after walking a mile from her boarding place, did not provide an atmosphere conducive to study. She boarded with a family whose small house was so open that everything freezable suffered from frost during the night. There was but one bed in the house and she slept with the wife in the bed while the husband slept with the children on the floor. Bread making under such environments required originality to make it a success. In such an atmosphere only dry yeast could be used. It would be started at noon and at night worked down hard and kept till morning when it would be set by the stove till it had risen enough to make into loaves and then it was baked. To keep it warm and from freezing at night the wife wrapped it up well and placed it in the bed at the teacher's feet.

Miss Eleanor Brown was teaching in Holt county at the time of the February 12, 1888, blizzard. Her family had moved to Madison county, Nebraska, in 1887 to profit by the better farming land. Miss Brown became teacher in School District 52 in Madison county in the spring of 1888 when the schools were going through evolution from the sod house period to the modern standard improved country school buildings. District 52 had reached the board shanty age when she became its teacher and had a board shanty much like the first one built in the county that was built in 1871 on the town site of what later became the county seat of Madison county. Miss Brown later married Mr. C. S. Snyder, a prominent business man and capitalist in Madison, the county seat of Madison county. Many years later District 52 advanced till a modern standard school building had been completed by the district and was ready for dedication forty years after Mrs. Snyder taught her first term of school in the district. The patrons of the district had assembled for a formal dedication of the building. A program was rendered and a lunch was served. County Superintendent Alice Hall delivered an address dedicating the building as one properly lighted and seated and presented the standard plate dedicating it as approved with all scholastic requirements complied with. Mrs. Snyder, their former teacher, was the guest of honor and in demonstrating the evolution of the country schools and school houses, read the following instructive and educational paper:

"Forty years ago a young girl who had had a year's experience in teaching in Holt county, came to this district to teach. The building she came to, was a frame building with windows on three sides so that the children always faced the glaring light. The door opened directly into the room, with no vestibule. There was a small heating stove in which we burned soft coal and it gave us rosy cheeks, but cold backs and feet, and at night we buried our ink bottles in the ashes to keep the ink from freezing solid.

"This young girl, the teacher, wore high shoes, long skirt and waist with high neck and long sleeves and to protect her dress she wore a black sateen apron gathered full on the band. Her black hair was coiled high on her head.

"I signed my contract for three months at $30 a month and Mr. Eckman was the director. In those days we had a spring and winter term of three months each. Lizzie Hutchinson was the first child to greet me with 'I can spell *see*.' There were about fifteen enrolled that spring. Of these Robert and Herman Kuntz still live in the district and are prosperous farmers. The children were a happy group. At noon you could see them hurry with their lunch so as to have more time to play. In 1889 I taught both winter and spring terms of school, still we had only six months of school. The children must have been unusually bright and studious in those days to have made the splendid records that they have made. During the winter there were often thirty pupils enrolled. The big boys who worked all summer would attend school after the corn was husked.

"The next winter term I taught the home school, 'the Muffly school' as it was called. Miss Aggie Twiss taught this school. I was back again for the spring term of '91 and for the following winter term which had four months, also for the spring term following this, making four full years that I taught in this district.

"Many of you will remember the old wooden pail and how you carried the water from the Hoffman farm close by. We had one dipper and had to watch the boys and girls so that they would not pour back the water left in the dipper. You know it was hard work to carry water by the pail full and children were just as thirsty in those days as they are today.

"The seats were just ordinary seats, room for two but when crowded, we made it seat three. There were no window shades, no curtains and no pictures in this school room. The teacher was the janitor and built her own fires.

"About once a year we had scrubbing day, and all hands helped. Every desk was scoured, cobwebs swept, windows cleaned and the floor scrubbed until we felt it was nice enough to eat off of. The teacher's salary, thirty dollars a month, was considered big wages in those days. One winter term I boarded with Mrs. Hutchinson, but found the walk too far, (a mile and a half), when I had to have the room warm by 8:30. The three other winter terms, I boarded with the Bentleys, who lived in a small three room house. Mr. Bentley was a carpenter and was away from home most of the time. In this home there was but one bed room, long and narrow. Mrs. Bentley and I occupied the bed and the three children slept in the trundle bed, which was pulled out from under the foot of the bed. There was about two feet of space between the bed and the wall, and only one window in the room which was never opened that entire winter. Five of us slept under those conditions and not one of us was sick that winter or even suffered from a cold. How is that for hygiene?

"I paid all of $1.50 a week for my board and room. That meant that I went home after school each Friday and came back on Monday morning and brought my noon lunch. In the spring terms, I boarded at home and walked three and a half miles each morning and night to save that $1.50, which was high finance.

"Sometimes at the close of the year, we had the parents enjoy a picnic dinner in the school room. I remember distinctly that Mrs. Reynolds, who lived

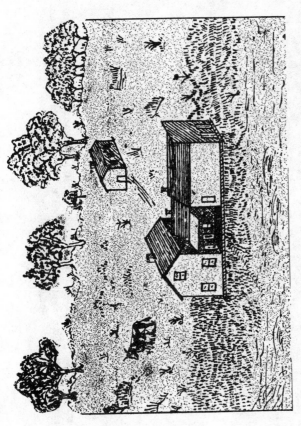

Madison City, county seat of Madison county, five years after the first homestead claim had been taken in the county. Note first frame house with first store attached to it. The family cow is seen lariated out to pasture. In back ground is the first school house built in Madison county. It was the property of school district No. 1. The lumber for these buildings was hauled 35 miles from the nearest railway station. Picture taken from a pen drawing made in 1871.

Standard country grade school building 1924. Full basement, furnace heated, sanitary light and seating. Plan approved by the state. Play ground in basement and hot lunches served pupils. All modern.

in the Blakely district but whose boys were attending school here that season, brought a big chicken pie that we all enjoyed. All brought abundantly and the cooks were as good in those days as today. An elaborate program was given at this time. This was the only big community affair in those days.

"We had a group picture taken of one of the terms and I have mine with me. We had no play apparatus but played andi-andi-over, pump, pump pull away, drop the handkerchief and such games, the teacher oftimes joining in these games. As much enthusiasm was shown in these games as is shown today in football or basketball games. Two years in succession we planted trees brought from my father's farm but no care was given them during the summer and they perished.

"As I look back through these passing years and picture that group of children who trooped into that building, there comes to me many a happy memory, not only with these children but with the parents and the school officers. The parents were not too busy but that they often invited the teacher into their homes and how I did appreciate it. What good times we had in those early days in our simple homes. That was genuine hospitality. The school officers were interested in the welfare of the children and showed this interest by coming to our programs.

"The children of those early days were bright, attractive boys and girls. I love to think back and picture them as I knew them then. I have watched them in later life and it has been a source of great satisfaction to see them develop into manhood and womanhood.

"Some of the girls taught school, some married and later I visited them in their homes; a few of the boys are active in business and others are following in the footsteps of their fathers, and are active farmers.

"Nothing pleases me more than to be with you tonight and I rejoice in the progressive spirit of this district that has made this beautiful building possible."

A picture reproduced from a pen drawing shows the entire town of Madison, Nebraska, that later became the county seat. It was made in 1871, five years after the arrival of the first permanent settler in the county. It shows the first home and the first store building to occupy the town site. It shows the first public school house made in the county for use of the pupils of School District No. 1. The school house is seen a short distance from the rest of the town. The family cow is shown in the background restrained from roaming by a long lariat rope.

An English emigration agent made an extended visit and minute examination of the new state, visiting most of the organized counties, all in eastern Nebraska, in 1876, and reported truthfully what he saw. The object of his visit was to report what English emigrants might find of value were they to become citizens of the state. He published his findings in a book he designated, "Nebraska, its Resources, Advantages and Drawbacks." He mentioned that Lincoln was six years old and had several thousand population and was going strong. That the university building was larger than would be required for many years. He referred to the original building with the filigree iron work top that stood in the center of the campus facing town. Comparing the educational buildings during the seventies with those fifty years later the Englishman would have been astounded. He would have considered the advancement of educational activities in the state as miraculous. He would have seen a wonderful country school system, exceptionally good grade and high schools in town, the normal schools, the junior colleges, the great number of immense buildings on an enlarged campus, experimental farms with schools of agricultural instruction, a large athletic field with its stadium seating 7,000 people, its fraternity buildings, the denominational universities that instruct thousands of young people each year, an incomparable state house costing $15,000,000, many homes and churches of beautiful design; all this would no doubt cause him to pause and exclaim, "See what God hath wrought!" He noted the state house that served the state in 1876 and described it as an not altogether unsuccessful attempt of an English architect to produce a building more ugly than certain English buildings in the old country.

It was not entirely the rich soil and good climate that wrought such wonders. They had been there for ages waiting for people to possess them. It was not the capital that sought profitable investment, not alone the brainy and courageous professional men and women who first established homes along the Missouri river. It was not alone the brave frontiermen who pushed the Indians and buffalo back to make way for homes of prosperous white people. They all helped to prepare the way.

It was the common people who reduced the prairie sod to a condition to permit raising crops. It was those who lived in dugouts, in sod houses, suffered hardships, endured privations during the probationary period from the admission of Nebraska as a state in 1867 to 1897 when it left its pioneer condition and joined the union as a full fledged state and took a place among the older and more prosperous commonwealths of the republic. It was the country teachers, daughters of the homesteaders who started Nebraska on the road to educational development. It was not the great minds of superior intellects of individuals that wrought such wonders in so short a time. It was done by a class of people composed of representatives of many nations that occupied and improved the eastern third of Nebraska. It was the composite fruit of the human melting pot that made the typical Nebraskan. Nebraska was made to blossom by the common people. Of these, the Nebraska pioneer country teachers must be given a high seat in the chariot of progress.

Mr. Whittaker, who participated in the military expedition against the predatory Indians in the Elkhorn river valley in 1859, when a treaty of peace was made with them at a point in Madison county where the town of Battle Creek was later located, made the claim that his first wife was the first common school teacher who taught in Nebraska. J. Sterling Morton while preparing his History of Nebraska denied Mr. Whittaker's claim, saying that to his personal knowledge there were several teachers "harbored" and actively teaching at the Presbyterian mission at Bellevue, south of Omaha at the time Mr. Whittaker said his wife was teaching in Omaha.

CHAPTER X

Railroad Land Grants
Taxes—Free Passes

"Besides granting public lands to actual settlers, Congress gave vast tracts of the public domain to the states for educational purposes. Between 1862 and 1871 Congress granted to railroad corporations 135,800,000 acres of land to encourage railroad construction. This large acreage would equal the area of the thirteen colonies at the time of the Revolutionary War, excluding the Carolinas. In 1860 there was 30,600 miles of railroads in the United States. There were but 52,856 miles in 1870."

THE gifts of public lands made by the United States Government to aid construction of railroads and to the state of Nebraska to encourage education were very liberal. It was recognized that such great gifts were for the purpose of speeding up the occupancy of the prairies by actual settlers. Without means of transportation, the cultivation of the lands would be greatly delayed. The Union Pacific Railway Co. was given alternate sections on a strip of land extending the entire length of the state lying ten miles on each side of the road. The grant amounted to over 11,000,000 acres. Stephen A. Douglas was credited with originating the land grant system.

The Burlington & Missouri Railway Co. in Nebraska was also given a land grant of alternate sections lying along their right of way in the southeastern part of the state but did not find land enough to make their quota and were permitted to go north of the Union Pacific grant and take alternate sections in counties north of the Platte river. These

(125)

grants came from the U. S. government. The government made liberal grants to the state and the state used most of the allowance to encourage education. The State University was allotted great tracts of land. Common education received two sections of school land in each township.

Besides land grants to encourage railroad building, taxpayers voted bonds in most of the voting precincts through which a railroad was built and gave to the railroads. The location of town sites was influenced by gifts of depot grounds, sometimes given by the owner of the land on which the station was located, and sometimes by the citizens subscribing to a fund to pay for the ground which they gave the railroad town site company.

The railroads sold their lands at low prices and gave liveral terms for paying. The sections alternating with their grants were taken by homesteaders. The numerous and profligate granting of public lands to aid different undertakings looked wasteful but time showed the wisdom of it in many ways. The Pawnee Indian reservation was relinquished by the Indians and sold for very low prices to settlers and speculators alike.

The large grant to the B. & M. road in Nebraska became the cause of a quarrel between the settlers in Boone county and the railroad. Settlers looked on the railroads, especially those to whom favors had been shown, as their oppressors. A homestead or other government claim was not liable for taxation till after the patent had been issued and it was sometimes eight years before the homesteader paid any taxes, while the railroad land was subject to taxation from the first. The sentiment prevailed

among settlers that the railroads and the speculators, as those who bought land for speculation or to
make a home later were called, should be taxed more
than those who lived on their land and endured
pioneer hardships.

The B. & M. Railway company offered their lands
for sale on long time payments. The common plan
was ten years time with first payment in five years
and 6 per cent annual interest. A discount of 25
per cent was given for cash. The land was listed
according to location or smoothness at from $2.00
to $5.00 an acre, the average being about $3.00. The
settlers were practically exempt from paying taxes.
Their homestead claims were not taxable, liberal
exemptions were allowed on personal property, and
a tax rebate was allowed by law for forest trees
planted and cultivated on taxable land. High valua-
tions were appraised against railroad and non-resident owned land for taxation purposes. Some school
district levies on railroad and non-resident property
exceeded the legal limit.

The railroads could not sell their land, partly because of the tax liens against them, nor would they
pay the taxes. In 1877 the B. & M. company owed
Boone county in taxes around $60,000, a part
illegally assessed. The tax quarrel injured both
county and railroad and a settlement did not seem
possible. The nearest railroad point was Columbus,
about fifty miles from Albion, the county seat.

During the year 1877 Adam Smith, an experienced promoter and a man of good judgment, came
in from the east and negotiated a settlement between the county and the railroad company whereby the county was to remit the taxes and receive
in return a graded wagon road running straight

southeast along the second bottom of the Beaver Creek valley to Genoa, the Pawnee agency location, and thence south to Silver Creek, a station on the Union Pacific railroad. It was reported that the B. & M. road gave him all their lands for effecting a settlement but they probably made him liberal concessions only, or gave him a stated number of acres. A popular meeting of the taxpayers was called at Albion to advise the county commissioners what action to take. The county had no railroads and a straight graded wagon road to market appealed to the people and with the proposition was an implied promise that the wagon road would be used for a railroad right-of-way at some time in the future. They did not realize that railroads prefer a first bottom and follow the water level along streams, which the first road that was built to Albion later did.

The county commissioners did not appear to have any legal right to remit taxes unless it was proven that they had been illegally assessed, and no such claim was raised. But the settlement was made by public acclaim of taxpayers in mass meeting convened. The meeting agreed, with few dissenting voices, to approve of the county commissioners making the settlement by remitting the taxes and accept from Adam Smith the graded wagon road in full payment. Mr. Smith made the road at trifling cost and all land owners gave the right of way angling through their valuable lands, some of which during inflation war times sold for $300 to $400 an acre.

An injunction was asked of the United States District Court in Omaha restraining the county from ever collecting the back taxes. Loran Clark

and others asked the court for an order restraining
the county commissioners from remitting the taxes.
They did not appear at the time set for the hearing and judgment was rendered against the county
by default. The temporary restraining order
against the county ever collecting the taxes was
made permanent.

Some time later an ambitious lawyer obtained a
contract from another board of commissioners to
collect the back taxes and interest that had now
amounted to $75,000.00, for one-fourth what was
collected. He was to bear all the expense of the
suit and receive nothing unless he was successful.
Suit was commenced, but as the lawyer could not
raise the expense money the county advanced it to
him. What was worse, they made it a cash item,
a creature of their own brain, and took it illegally
from the county treasury. An allowed account
against the general fund of the county at the time
had to wait nearly two years before its turn came
for payment. The suit had gone through the United
States district court at Omaha and was appealed to
the United States supreme court at Washington.

The case came up for hearing during my first
year as county commissioner. My predecessor had
been the chief supporter of the attempted collection
and in advancing money to pay expenses, contrary
to agreement. The lawyer to whom was given the
collectors contract engaged General Cowin, a prominent Omaha lawyer, to present the case to the U. S.
Supreme Court at Washington for him, and the
county was asked to remit about $1,350 to pay for
the brief or be nonsuited. It happened that one
of the commissioners was unable to attend the meeting and a deadlock occurred. The other commis-

sioner was strong for sending the money and I was
firmly against it. My contention was that the district court had granted a perpetual injunction
against collecting the taxes and it had been further
clinched by the default of the county in the restraining suit by Loran Clark. The issue of the right of
the county to remit the taxes as they did, had not
been raised. The judge who presided at the U. S.
District Court when the perpetual injunction had
been granted was now a member of the Supreme
Court and would not be likely to advise a change.
I further contended that we could not legally order
the cash taken from the depleted treasury to pay
for the brief or for any purpose.

This brought another popular taxpayers meeting.
I was advised by nearly every person that called
to agree to the request. Lawyers, bankers, business
men and preachers all advised me to recede. Only
one man sustained me. I looked upon the winning
of the suit as absolutely impossible and bad policy
for a county that was struggling to get on a paying
basis to risk good money in what seemed a hopeless
case. The next day the sick commissioner was
brought in and the "cash item" was allowed. The
case was presented and we were beaten. About
$3.50 of the $1,350, sent to pay for the brief was
returned to us.

The case was probably the most important and
far reaching of any case the commissioners ever
had to deal with. It differed from the popular
meeting that supported the commissioners in settling the taxes. Had the county won, my reputation as a business man would have been ruined.

A precedent was established by the taxpayers in
advising settlement when no law approved the way

they did it. It might have been common law or a reversal to the New England town meetings. At the time, it looked like an enormous price to pay for the grading of the road and the few bridges made, but time demonstrated that it was a wonderfully good investment. A diagonal wagon road, that was later made into a state road, was established. Efforts to change to section lines have usually failed. It is a wonderful asset to the county and a benefit to the public.

Title to the land was settled and settlers came in and Adam Smith sold the land on the terms and at the prices fixed by the B. & M. Railroad. In 1879 the Union Pacific road proposed to build branches north to Norfolk and northwest to Albion in Boone county. They asked the counties along the proposed line to vote them bonds. Boone county did and all complied except Platte county, but the bonds were defeated by Columbus. They had all the trade from the northwest and a railroad there would cut off that trade. Therefore they refused to vote bonds. Union Pacific Railway officials were offended. Jay Gould, one of the prominent officials of the road, made a speech from the rear of his private car in Columbus, threatening to make grass grow in the streets of Columbus because of the antagonism of the people in not voting bonds. The branch road was started from a side track a few miles west of Columbus and built across the Loup river and extended to Norfolk in 1879 and to Albion in 1880, thus cutting off Columbus as a junction. The first winter saw the ice in the Loup river take out the railroad bridges, and towns beyond were without service till the track could be graded and rails laid from Columbus.

All the railroad contentions were of vital importance to the settlers and the administration of railroad affairs became more important politics than
what was being done at Washington.

One of the activities of the railroad politicians,
"railroad cappers" the people called them, was to
influence delegates and control nominating conventions. The most effective way for the railroad
managers to control county and state conventions
and legislation by state legislatures was by issuing
free railroad passes over the railroads to convention delegates and members of state legislatures.
Both leading national parties profited by it and
shrewd manipulators of a campaign to secure favorable legislation for their roads, treated both parties
impartially, with the view that in any event they
would have the winner on their side. It was one
of the war cries of the Populists in 1890 that the
legislatures and office holders were bought with
passes. Before state conventions a leader in each
county would be given a blanket pass to and from
the convention in which the convention was held
that would enable him to pass his whole delegation
without expense to the delegates themselves so far
as transportation was concerned. Most leaders of
all parties held annual passes over all roads in the
state and many of them over the whole system in
other states. Even Populist leaders, whose followers
objected to the pass system rode on passes and
resorted to subterfuge to deceive their party sup-
porters.

During the antimonopoly party crusade of the
eighties the cry against buying support for railroad
abuses by giving free passes, arose loud and deep.
Senator Van Wycke, who profited by the opposition

to railroad influence by a six year term in the
United States senate, made the excuse for riding on
railroad passes by claiming that he was foraging off
the enemy. Leaders who accepted pass favors from
the railroad cappers, or members of the legislature
who accepted passes were accused of having been
"bought" by the enemies of the people.

The applications for free passes over railroads
and city street car lines by public officials, business
men and those who might plead that they had influence became a great scandal. In time it also became
an annoyance to railway managers who came to
doubt its value to them. They did not object to giving free passes where a reasonable prospect of receiving service in return was manifest, but there
were many applicants for free rides who were of
doubtful value. Usually by ingenuous pleading the
applicant was made the beneficiary and secured his
rides free. The annoyance finally became so great
that the transportation companies themselves joined
in the movement to abolish the giving of free passes.
At best it was a graft of doubtful value in most
cases.

As an example of the way the campaign was carried out by individuals to secure free rides over a
transportation system, the experience of a deputy
sheriff might be given. The officer was obliged to
pay out much money while traveling in his line of
duty serving papers. He complained that it caused
him trouble to list his claim for mileage and make
his report and secure receipts from conductors and
ticket agents for money paid out to enable him to
have his expense account allowed. Of course, if he
could secure a free pass he could still make his

reports and collect his travel expenses and it would go hand in hand with the pass. Therefore he approached the superintendent of the road with a request for free transportation and was promised that his application would be considered.

After waiting a reasonable time and the pass not being forthcoming he mentioned his receptive mood for a pass again, and again he was assured that the matter would have earnest consideration. But the free pass did not ride and he seemed to be no nearer the attainments of his hopes than before. The third time he applied and the superintendent noting his persistence decided that he could not stall any longer and inquired, "Really, Mr. Johnson, what reason can you give why our road should pass you free, or what service have you ever rendered our system that we should grant you this favor?"

The applicant was equal to the occasion and answered, "I don't know a blankety, blank reason for asking for the pass on the ground that I have performed any service to justify my riding on your road without paying for it, but there are some things I have left undone that I should have done that seems to me warrants you in giving me the pass. For instance when I have seen your agents and the cappers of your road tampering with witnesses and jurors when you had cases in court, I failed to arrest them and shut them up in jail as I should have done." The argument seemed to carry weight and the superintendent quickly saw the light and responded, "Well, well, Mr. Johnson we will see what can be done about it?" He went into the next room and returned with an annual pass that was very satisfying to the deputy sheriff.

CHAPTER XI

Live Stock and Grain Dealers

"Whosoever could make two ears of corn, or two blades of grass, to grow upon a spot of ground where only one grew before, would deserve better of mankind, and do more essential service to his country, than the whole race of politicians put together."—Swift.

I WAS fortunately located in an eastern central Nebraska county, about 100 miles west of Omaha. The people were truly representative of the citizenship of the state at large. They were strong, active men and women, few exceeding forty years of age. A very few above sixty years had joined the exodus from states farther east, hoping with the younger ones to secure a free home on the rich Nebraska prairies. Among the settlers were people who had been engaged in trade, mechanics or educational work. They became land hungry and took Horace Greeley's advice to "Go West." These people promptly set about securing schools, churches and Sunday schools. They engaged in politics and Boone county, made up of a mixture of all nationalities, with the American born predominating, and a good sprinkling of Irish, were able to accomplish almost anything. Many had followed neighbors to the new country. In one corner of the county a large body of American born Germans bought homes close together. In another, Norwegians from Minnesota followed the first family to locate, and bought cheap land or homesteaded near each other. A number of Irish-American families from the same neighborhood in Wisconsin

(135)

exerted a profound influence on the activities of the new county. A colony of Swedes established homes together in the eastern part near the county line.

It required someone in town to buy the grain and live stock of the farmers and sell them feeder cattle and coal. In this particular county those engaged in this line of activities were largely of Irish or Scotch-Irish descent, or were examples of the early melting pot of emigrants who had left the British Isles. In our county they were red-blooded, live men. They were public spirited to the most unselfish degree and would submit to being bled white to help the general community or help someone in trouble. But they would fight each other in business and politics to the finish. Even a close friend would not be immune from a thorough trimming in a case of buying or selling of grain, coal, hay or live stock, or when a candidate for office. There was nothing narrow about them, neither could they be classed as the most devout in religion, or very ambitious prohibitionists Being in the thirties, or early forties, they looked to the future optimistically and the time for accounting for their sins, distant. Many of their questionable acts were committed more in a spirit of bravado and sport. Most of them after filling their allotted places in life, passed away leaving a younger generation to take up their work in a different way, more in accord with the growth of the state.

In our county seat town, Barney was a lone wolf broker in hay, milch cows, feeder steers and feeder pigs. That meant young cattle fit to put in a feed lot to finish with corn and hay and the pigs the right size to clear up what the cattle left, and when mature ship to the Omaha or Chicago market.

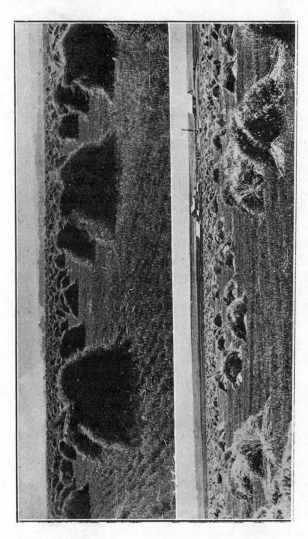

Nebraska Wheat Fields. Reproduced from a photograph. Not freak fields but typical of Nebraska soil fertility when the ground is properly tilled.

Sheep fattening yards. Thousands were annually brought from pasture ranges in the sand hills of western Nebraska or from the mountains to finish for market on corn in the sod house district.

Barney did not stoop to open falsehoods to sell his wares but the door was easily opened at times. Having a fresh cow that looked as though she would yield milk abundantly, a buyer asked Barney how much milk she gave. He responded, "As much as she can; go and milk her yourself and see." The buyer got a big pail full of milk and bought the cow. In a few days he came back complaining that the cow never yielded anywhere near as much milk after the first milking. Barney inquired how often he milked her and the answer was that he had followed the usual custom of twice a day. "That," Barney said, "is all that is the matter. Heretofore the cow had been milked but twice a week."

Barney sold prairie hay. A customer who was unfortunately slow pay, desired hay for his horse. He asked the price and Barney answered, "For cash $9.00 a ton, and on time $5.00." An explanation was asked and the prospective buyer was told that it was to reduce the loss in selling hay to slow paying customers, that the low price was made when the hay was charged.

Fitz and Tom were veteran live stock and grain buyers. They also sold Rock Springs coal and jobbed feeder cattle, pigs and sheep and bought and shipped fat cattle and hogs to the packing houses. At one time they had a lot of western sheep that they had brought in to be finished on corn. An English born stock feeder having a large farm just outside town, who frequently became a competitor of Fitz and Tom, wanted to buy the sheep to add to his feed lot herd. Fitz said to Tom, "It is all right to let this old son-of-a-gun have the sheep but we must raise a little on him. He will be along tomorrow to weigh them up. Early tomorrow

morning we will drive the flock down the lane and
through the creek and enough water will stay in
the wool to enable us to make a good honest profit
on the flock." So the sheep got a march through
the creek and the unsuspecting buyer took the flock,
water and all, home with him and put them in his
feed lot. After feeding them the allotted time he
shipped the sheep to market and they weighed less
than when he had put them on full feed several
months before. He learned how he had been hooked
but kept his counsel and waited an opportunity to
get even.

Fitz and Tom had the sympathies of another stock
dealer and all the employes around both yards. The
sheep deal was looked on as good business. The
man who had bought the water with the sheep
finally matured a big yard of cattle valued at many
thousand dollars. A broker buying them at a price
that left a margin would naturally be ambitious to
buy the whole lot. The owner began negotiations
with the combined lot of local cattle feeders to buy
his yard of cattle. The better to complete a transfer it was customary to discuss it in a saloon, and
take frequent libations of old rye for luck till a
proper condition would be reached to make a deal.
Abe, the Englishman, used the rye very sparingly
himself but plied the others with it in a most prodi-
gal manner. As a result, he got them into such
a genial state of mind that he made a contract to
sell the stock to the syndicate for a good bit more
than they would bring on the market. The agreement was to weigh them up next day.

Next day came and Abe knew that when sober
the syndicate would realize that they were paying
dearly for driving the sheep through the creek, and

would use every device to make the bulk price on the fat cattle lower by under weighing, making erroneous entries of weights, and that he was up against a bunch who knew their business. He came to me and urged that I attend to the weights and figures because he was weak in mathematics but could handle the smart alecks in everything else. I helped him and made them both hew to the line and checked several attempts to make it otherwise. The cattle buyers in this conflict lost more than Abe had lost on his sheep and the incident was closed.

In 1894 a complete grain crop failure compelled taking all the live stock out of the country. Succeeding years brought bumper grain crops. There was no live stock in the country to eat the corn or consume the forage. Stock cattle were shipped in from other states to pasture the corn stalks and winter over on the oat, wheat and flax straw on the farms. John and Sam who were live stock brokers negotiated with an Iowa party to take a large herd of stock cattle, mixed cows and steers of mixed ages, and herd them on stalk fields and straw stacks from early winter to April. The cattle arrived in due time and were sent to the country and herded. Later, John and Sam negotiated to buy the cattle, and a contract was signed to buy the whole herd and pay for them at the time in the spring set for delivery.

Of course a careful check was kept on the herd and they were frequently counted. It was apparent that the herd was short one animal. Eventually it was determined that a cow having a crumpled horn was absent from the flock. Being aware of human nature as possessed by stockmen, they suspected that the Iowa man was guilty of trying to hold out on them in some way. A search of all the farms and feed lots for miles around was made, and the cow was found in possession of a farmer ten miles away who had bought her of the Iowa man after he had sold the herd under contract to John and Sam. That was a serious violation of law and custom and an exceedingly unwise undertaking, especially as it was but a small item of the sale.

It was agreed to keep quiet about the loss of the cow and complete the contract and make an adjustment when the time for the transfer came in the spring. Accordingly, the Iowa man showed up at the appointed time and John, who was a widower, and Sam, a bachelor, habitually did much night entertainment among themselves at the office, met the visitor and had all their helpers present. An early day stag party was put on with cold chicken, abundance of Anheuser-Busch suds, rye whiskey and cigars. The feasting and conviviality continued throughout the night. A game of poker was on, to which all set in for small stakes. It was purely a social affair where genial spirits met, and enjoyed themselves.

But an end always comes and as the train left early in the morning for Omaha, along toward morning the Iowa man suggested that as the night was passing, it would be well to get down to business and check up. John, as spokesman, inquired frigidly, "To what business do you refer, sir?" Of course the answer was that it was to complete the contract for the herd of cattle and get his pay.

John responded, "There is no settlement to make, sir. You have forfeited the cattle and we are going to send you to the penitentiary for stealing a cow from us." The social affair was all over and all looked the part that John threatened. The man was alarmed and nonplussed. It really looked like a severe punishment to take the herd and send the owner to the penitentiary for rustling one cow and one of the firm's assistants suggested mercy and leniency for that reason. That if they kept the cattle for the offense, that the man should not be sent to prison. It was finally so agreed and the herd stayed to allay the wounded feelings of John and Sam and their helpers, and the man gladly relinquished claim and left town. I was given these details by a helper who was an eye witness and present at the adjustment. It was an example of early day justice as administered by stock men themselves. They even considered it a practical joke.

Once the popular hotel keeper where Fitz and Tom boarded had a young male pig among a lot of hogs he was feeding from the hotel refuse. On my farm I had a large hog that had been a fixture there for some time and I suggested to the landlord that he trade his little hog to me for my big one. This landlord was one of the finest big hearted men to be found anywhere. He made the trade and sent my big hog to Fitz and Tom's shipping yard. In a couple of days he asked his two boarders to give him a check for his hog and they coolly declined to pay, alleging that another hog killed the landlord's hog in a fight shortly after it was brought to the yards. The landlord got no check. It was such little love taps that the red blooded pioneers dealt out to each other. David Harum's golden rule was their interpretation of it. "Do unto others as others would do unto you, but do it to them fust."

Once my brother-in-law who was my partner on the farm, brought in two wagon loads of fat hogs, mixed sizes, and sold them to the buyer who worked for Fitz and Tom. The hogs were weighed in lots of four or five at once and the prices were different. I was soon called to the yards because weights had been shortened. Before my arrival, Tom, who was an inveterate joker and 100 per cent Irish, had the hogs weighed over and corrected the weights to benefit us fifteen or twenty dollars. Tom was sagely advising his buyer in the presence of my brother-in-law as to what was prudent in weighing stock. He was soberly saying as I came up, "Now, Bill, when you have been in the hog and cattle business as long as I have you will learn to know better than to attempt to swipe more than 150 to 200 pounds at a draft." What could Bill say when his boss instructed him against stealing weights in excess when his mistake had made each draft three or four hundred pounds under weight and the seller believing that he had purposely been attempting to short weight him.

Sometimes a merchant would put on a buyer to buy grain to stimulate their own trade or merchants in the part of town away from the shipping sidetrack, hoping to divert trade to their side of town, would engage an inexperienced man to buy grain and they would furnish shovelers. It was a delight for the experienced dealers to get the green buyer to mix a load of rye with his wheat, or barley with the oats.

Sometimes the farmer had a comeback on the grain buyers. My first year there, was when the first corn crop of any size had been harvested and a great tonnage of shell corn had to be freighted out. Farmers gladly contracted their crop for 25 cents a bushel and considered that the corn having been produced on ten dollar an acre land they thought they were in luck. However, the average price soon went up to 42 cents because of a shortage of the crop in other states. An old German farmer, one of the few above forty years of age, contracted his corn to a town grain buyer for 25 cents a bushel but before delivering it, the price went up and stayed around 42 cents. He was grieved and no argument could induce him to deliver the corn on his contract. Finally the exasperated buyer said to him, "If you agree that you are a dam old skunk and a liar, I will call the contract off." Quickly the old man responded: "I bees a dam old skunk and liar." This closed the incident and the treaty of peace was observed by both sides and friendship was restored.

All the buyers claimed to be the farmers' friends. The farmers considered that the buyers were their rank enemies and this belief was one of the means of starting several farmers organized movements in the state. They would even charge that Fitz would weigh a wagon that drove on his scales and send the driver to the coal bins to get coal and weigh back on his return without looking to see if he had coal on his wagon. He was charged with calling a net load of coal 800 pounds when the man had looked at the coal and declined to take any. Another coal dealer once announced while he was "lit up" that he was the farmers friend because he gave them 1,700 pounds of coal for a 2,000 pound ton while Fitz only gave them 1,300 pounds.

This competition did not exist always where the people were of one nationality but this county was typical of the class that bought and sold live stock, grain and coal in the state prior to 1897. They were ruinously unwise in competition and as a rule went broke in the end. Once while I directed the buying of grain at the milling plant on the Northwestern railroad, Fitz and a German competitor bought on the Union Pacific. I paid no attention to them but paid 13 cents for oats and had a profit margin of one quarter cent. Fitz and his competitor pooled and agreed not to pay above 12 cents. One day Fitz's buyer told me the oat market was booming on their side of town. The Dutchman had bought a load of oats for fifteen and a half and the Scotchman one for a quarter cent better. They broke their agreement when Fitz discovered that his opponent had bought a load of oats for twelve and a half cents. When accused of his perfidy he denied buying a bushel that day for over twelve cents. When told who the man was he bought of and the price he paid he excused it by saying, "Well, that was bought after night."

To explain why he could not give credit for coal, Fitz had this poem in large type displayed on the wall of his office—

"To trust is to bust,
To bust is hell.
No trust, no bust,
No bust, no hell."

One of the most prominent and successful men in the county became wealthy handling his farms and feeding cattle and hogs and buying horses and mules to ship to market. For a time he had associated

with him a young man who later made a great success importing horses from Germany and Belgium
prior to the World war. While a boy, he engaged
as a clerk in a relative's department store, although
his family occupation was the handling of live stock
and practiced by his forbears for several previous
generations. I was reliably informed that this boy
saved enough from his wages as clerk to buy a cow.
Then he traded the cow for a good looking horse
that had a distinctive blemish on the front of its
face that greatly damaged its sale value. He covered the blemish with a wide strap and paraded the
horse up the street in front of the stable where the
buyer was assembling horses for shipment. His
efforts were rewarded and the horse was sold. Next
day, after the stable men had revealed the discov-
ery of the blemish, the buyer called the boy for
an explanation. "Did you know that blemish was
there?" he was asked. He answered, "Yes, do you
see that wide strap. It cost me a dollar and a half
to fix that halter to hide the blemish." Then the
good judgment of the buyer dispelled his anger. He
hired the boy to work for him and kept him as long
as he could induce him to work for wages.

But all these men, no matter what their lapses
or practical jokes in dealing with associates in business, had great big sympathetic hearts and would
always help liberally in case of sickness or disaster
and were always broadminded and helpful in public
matters. Their shortcomings were of their age, environments and common custom. They were not
hypocritical and they certainly filled a place in making the melting pot of our great state boil and
bubble.

CHAPTER XII

District Courts
During the Eighties

"It doth appear, you are a worthy judge. You know the law, your exposition hath been most sound: I charge you by the law whereof you are a well deserving pillar, proceed to judgment."—Shakespeare.

THE nightmare of the busy merchant or farmer is the fear of being called to perform jury service at district court sessions. The district court is next to the supreme court in rank, and to it is referred most of the state equity and criminal cases for trial. The most active men are usually named from whom to select the regular jury. There are always retired farmers or mechanics temporarily without work, who are willing to serve as jurymen, and being in the full possession of their faculties, and minds at rest, make better jurymen than a busy farmer or merchant whose mind is distracted by his own business cares from the evidence introduced at the trial.

Being a physician I was not called for jury work till late in the eighties when I served as juryman in two interesting jury trials. At the time I was giving my attention to editing and publishing a county newspaper. An interesting trial had been called at district court wherein a man had been charged with selling liquor without a license, and expecting to gather a good report for my paper, I ventured into the court room while the jury was being selected. Eleven jurymen had been chosen and to my surprise I was called. I plead ill health, that I was a physician, a fireman and had expressed an opinion on the case both editorially and in discussion. The late Judge Albert was attorney for the accused man and the county attorney appeared for the state. Both smiled audibly at my defense and both accepted me in spite of my excuses.

The case was where a man had been charged with keeping a "speak-easy" or "hole in the wall" in a neighboring town and four indictments had been lodged against him for selling intoxicants. He had been previously tried on one count, the other three having been withdrawn by the state after the trial was called. The man had been found not guilty because witnesses who testified to drinking his liquor swore that they did not know what spiritus frumenti was and did not know what they had been served with. He was liberated and the county attorney had now brought him to trial on the three counts previously withdrawn. After the jury was sworn and the three indictments read, Mr. Albert asked that the accused man be discharged because he had been in jeopardy on the three counts when they had been dropped at the first trial. The judge overruled the objection and ordered the trial to proceed.

The first witness was a prosperous farmer who swore that while he had been served different drinks at the place he did not know what he was drinking, neither did he know what spiritus frumenti was. He was following the evidence of the witness in the first trial. No questioning could bring

from him the admission that he had bought and
drank either whiskey or beer in the "speak-easy."

At this stage the judge broke in with, "Mr.
Sheriff, take that witness to jail and keep him on
bread and water till his memory gets better." It
had a marvelous effect upon the witness and his
mentality visibly improved till in a short time he
swore positively to the nature of the drink furnished
him by the defendant. The other two counts resulted as the first one did. The counsel made their
pleas, the jury was instructed and retired for de-
liberation.

There were several drinking men on the jury who
had been gladly accepted by the defense. One man
spoke the sentiments of all when he said he knew
enough about whiskey and beer to think that if the
witness got what satisfied him that he had been
served with what the defendant was charged with
selling. The county attorney had hoped to get a
conviction on but one count but the jury returned
a verdict of guilty in all three counts. Judge Albert
took an appeal to the supreme court on the grounds
that the court lacked jurisdiction because the defendant had been in jeopardy on the same counts
before. Pending action by the supreme court the
defendant went to jail on a stiff fine sentence im-
posed by the trial judge.

The supreme court took its time and eventually
acted and overruled the lower court and found for
Judge Albert's client but he had already served his
fine in jail. He did not crave another trial.

Another time I was called on the jury just as I
was in the bootleg case. No plea or reason I gave
would suffice to excuse me. The case was one where

an old time Nebraskan who had served as a private soldier during the Civil war and Nebraska Indian wars in the Second Nebraska volunteers, was charged with manhandling a Bohemian woman. The old veteran lived on a homestead and the woman, who was single, had filed on an adjoining claim and with her mother was holding the claim. The two homesteaders got into a neighborly quarrel and the woman came out to the fire guard line where the old man was plowing and fired an old army musket at him heavily loaded with bird shot. The gun fire did no damage but he caught her and gave her a good beating with his cane and she had him haled into court to answer to a charge of assault with intent to do great bodily injury.

On that jury were two men who could have been good jurymen but being temporarily out of employment had been "sticking" juries by failing to decide on the evidence till after the jury had been taken to the hotel for supper and had held out in the evening long enough to count another day's jury service.

The evidence introduced showed clearly that the beating had been given the woman but did not show extenuating circumstances enough to justify him in being so thorough about it. The jury determined that he was guilty but misunderstood the instructions to mean that if found guilty as charged, the old veteran must go to jail. Had it been a fine and he chose to go to jail rather than pay the fine, we would have agreed. We went into court and asked the judge to enlighten us as to the difference and he told us it was none of our business but to retire and deliberate on the evidence. Of course the judge's blunt answer did not please a jury of American citizens trying one of their fellow citizens.

I argued the evidence and the probable punishment to be meted out and all but the two hard boiled jurymen agreed with me. They soon showed that they intended to follow their old game. For myself I was opposed to sending a veteran of the Civil war to jail where both parties had been to blame. This was Tuesday forenoon and I called a bailiff and told him to go to the printing office and tell my employes that I would be gone all the week.

Court being in session, we were locked in a jury room ten by twelve feet in size. Eleven jurymen and the bailiff smoked. I did not smoke. There was one window and it was closed. We went to work and worked faithfully all day and at night were given the big court room and worked most of the night. Arguments would be made by the nine who wanted to get out badly and they would finally line up and be found arguing to me. I always responded that I was agreed, to go talk to the two who misunderstood the case. Lying down for a short sleep in the night one lone juryman, who had a bottle in his pocket, suffered the catastrophe of having the cork come out and all his stimulant run out on the floor.

Then the foreman, who was more elderly than the rest, asked me to have the bailiff take me to the drug store where I had formerly engaged in business, and get him some whiskey. I answered that I had heard him testify in court once that he did not know what whiskey was and I did not care to place him in the way of temptation at his age. He assured me that if I would go to the store and get liquid from the big shelf bottle that had a piece broken from its lip and assure him it came from that bottle, that he would fearlessly undertake to drink it. I still refused but gave him a dose of quinine and he was much strengthened thereby.

Finally after all that wrangling from noon one day, most of the night and again in that little stifling jury room, about 3 P. M. I found an old issue of the Nebraska statutes that should not have been in the room, and read passages to convince the two jury stickers. The argument was not strong but they accepted it with joy and we reached a verdict. Thus it can be seen how two obstinate jurymen can exhaust the rest of the jury. Had they been reasonable a verdict would have been arrived at at noon the first day.

In 1882 all territory west and northwest of Boone and Antelope counties was unorganized territory. The district had two judges and they were elected as political candidates. The democrats were in the minority but Judge Platte of Grand Island and Thomas Doyle, a young Greeley county attorney, too young to serve as judge, made a tour of the district to arouse interest to give them the democratic nomination. Judge Platte said he had great hopes of election because there were a great many horse thieves in the sandhills and on the Niobrara river and they were all democrats. In spite of their hopes they were defeated.

An Albion man who joined the gold rush to the Black Hills in South Dakota, told me that he was in Deadwood during the toughest of the time and was there the day Wild Bill Hickok was murdered while playing cards. "Wild Bill" was a noted char-

acter, much of his reputation having come from
eastern magazine articles prepared by reporters
who were unmercifully strung by the frontiersmen.
Still Bill was a real gun fighter and on this occasion
sat in on a poker game with his back to the door.
He had asked his partner to change places with him
as soon as the hand was played out because it was
against his custom, he said, to sit with his back to
the door. Before the hand was played, a man who
claimed that Bill had killed his brother, came in
and placed a gun at Bill's head and shot him dead.

My informant said that Deadwood was just at the
stage where the lawless element and those who desired law and order were ready to contend for
supremacy. The murderer escaped, but a coroner's
jury was formed to determine the cause of Bill's
death and the Albion man was chosen as one of
the jurymen. He said they met at night in the
celebrated old log town hall that served for such
trials as they had. All night the jury labored with
a howling, shooting, drunken mob surging around
the building. All the jurymen, except my informant, agreed that the murderer had killed Bill in self
defense. Finally a Winchester rifle barrel appeared
through a crack between the logs and inquiry was
made for the juryman who could not agree. Agreement came without further delay.

But the murder was the turning act between law-
lessness and orderly government. The murderer
was pursued and returned and afterward hanged for
the crime. Wild Bill began his career as a gunman
while employed near Fairbury in Nebraska to de-
fend one of the Overland stage stations and killed
a man named McCandlass and others. Later he

took the job to clean up bad towns which he did
by promptly shooting offenders. He was essentially
a Nebraska man and a Nebraska product. For a
time he was a member of Buffalo Bill's show company. During Indian wars he did a great deal of
scouting for the army and fought Indians following
the Civil war.

It was surprising how few minor crimes and mis-
demeanors early Nebraskans were charged with
compared with the towns in the lake region. But
murders that were unusual in the older country,
sometimes seem to become epidemic. A string of
five men charged with murder were once confined
in the Boone county jail when there was room for
but four and the last comer had to occupy the cor-
ridor.

The first one was where two 18-year-old boys
had been brought from England by the father of
one of them and were living on a farm near town,
went hunting birds one hot Sunday afternoon during the summer. The boy who was not related to
the family, and was of weak mentality, returned
alone and reported that he left the other boy during
the afternoon and had not seen him since. An all
night search found the missing boy in a sunflower
patch, dead from a gun shot wound that had entered the back of his neck and the charge of bird-
shot had lodged in his tongue. A coroner's jury
was convened and under their urging the suspected
killer admitted that the other boy accidentally shot
himself. In the meantime I had been operating in
a post mortem examination for the coroner and
found that the shot in the dead boy's tongue differed
from that in his own gun but corresponded with

the shot in the other boy's gun, and his guilt was established. Much sob talk and much sentiment was indulged in at the trial and the murderer was sent to prison for 15 years. Other murders followed. One man was sentenced to hang but got a new trial and was given a life sentence.

A man named Mike Lamb who lived in Greeley county, had long been acting as a reception committee for cattle stolen from the sandhill grazing land and farmers were afraid of him and his miscreants. Some years after the murder cases it happened occasionally that a tired herd of stolen cattle would reach Mike and he would cause them to be left in some one's pasture till they rested up. The owner of the pasture would fear to complain. A local priest who possessed a good pasture instructed the man in charge that if Mike Lamb undertook to occupy his pasture with stolen cattle to take a shotgun to him. Soon after, Mike and a cowboy drove in a herd of stolen cattle and the cowboy and caretaker became involved in a dispute. The cowboy threatened to use his revolver and the caretaker turned loose on him with one barrel of his shotgun and the cowboy's pony wheeled and turned the other side to the shotgun whereupon the cowboy got the other barrel in his other side, and fell off on the wire fence where he laid without molestation for about a day. Mike put spurs to his horse and escaped. One Irishman came to town and reported the excitement that followed the shooting and said that a mob was likely to organize to hang the man who did the shooting. I insisted that it would be wrong because the killer was defending the property left in his charge. That was not the trouble,

my informant said, it was because he wasted the
second barrel on the cowboy who already had plenty
instead of using it on Mike Lamb.

Another time Mike had sent in a herd of cattle
diseased with Texas itch and the excited settlers
drove them into the Cedar river and drowned most
of them. The bank in a nearby village was later
robbed in daylight by a young man working for
Mike. Eventually Mike, who was a noted criminal,
who who came from a respectable family, was sent
to the penitentiary for one of his many misdeeds.

CHAPTER XIII

Nebraska Politics

O, farmers of the western plain,
With prospects quite as fine as silk,
Who cuss the luck and pray for rain,
And keep more cows than you can milk."
—*Doc Bixby*

NEBRASKA was beset with politicians from its earliest settlement till after the period of aggressive populism and the dispersing of the national political parties by William Jennings Bryan. Indiana had been the most notorious political battlefield in the union but their battles were strictly along party lines. Let a single Hoosier change party affiliation in a township, and it was said that the farmers locked their hen houses till the reason for the overt act could be investigated. Elections were not changed by argument but by the campaign fund and the party that could pay most for votes was usually victorious.

Nebraska had a strong national republican political foundation, possibly because so many veterans of the Civil war had emigrated to the state and they were nearly all republicans. While national party lines were maintained, Nebraska politics was largely local and campaigns were fought bitterly by the brainy, courageous young men who first entered the territory or state. As an example of their candidness and earnestness in local politics, a resolution, written by young J. Sterling Morton, and adopted by a meeting of territorial electors at a public meeting is herewith given. It shows dis-

tinctly that they were displeased with their territorial governor. Herewith are the resolutions:

"Whereas: We believe that in order to attain the
ends of just government, executive power should
be vested in upright, honorable men; and, whereas,
we believe that that power, when confided to unprincipled knaves, who seek rather to control than consult the people, whom we recognize as the only true
sovereigns, is always used to the advantage of the
few and the oppression of the many, wherefore, Resolved, 1st, That Acting Governor Cuming is neither
an upright, honest nor honorable man. Resolved,
2nd, That he, the aforesaid Acting Governor Cuming, is an unprincipled knave, and he seeks to control rather than consult the people."

I was glad to get away from the Indiana national
politics and in 1882 undertook to do the caring for
the sick in Nebraska and give my partner freedom
to attend to the local politics of the state and county.
I was located in the county seat of Boone county.
State politics recognized national party leaders but
state and county political contentions were along
the lines of local color. Forgetting their common
party, republican state leaders battled between the
interests of the Union Pacific and B. & M. railroads.
As opposed to the railroads many republicans and
the democratic voters united to form the Antimonopoly party.

Edward Rosewater, a very able man, and one
who helped greatly in the development of Nebraska,
owned and edited the Omaha Bee, the first virile
daily newspaper published in Nebraska. He was
associated in leading antimonopoly politics, with
C. H. VanWycke, who had formerly been a repub-

lican congressman representing a New York district. The fight went to the uttermost parts of the state and was bitter, vindictive and hotly contested. My partner, Dr. D. A. Lewis, was the leader in our county. He was warmly assisted by A. D. Brainard, editor of the Albion Argus, and others nearly as active. A straight republican paper was maintained by A. W. Ladd, while Loran Clark and John Peters, two of the most astute republican politicians in the state, led the straight party.

The "Antimonops" struggled to capture the county convention and nominate county officers. At the county convention they had a few more delegates than the straight party had but some of the Anti delegations showed a disposition to listen to the voice of the tempter. The convention was called, and the credentials committee reported 36 delegates that the Antis claimed and 32 surely for the straight party. Thereupon the regulars joined in electing an Anti chairman, and convinced him that as chairman he had no vote, except in case of a tie.

John Peters had been county clerk for years. W. B. Daniels had been sheriff from the beginning and S. P. Bollman had been treasurer and was a fixture. The Antis desired to displace those veterans. The convention went to the mat on county clerk. Joe Haire came in with his delegation of five from Midland precinct. He, too, was counted with the Antis. He was a candidate for county sheriff himself. The regulars promised that if he would bring his squad into camp for Peters and Bollman that they would put him across for sheriff, against the old soldier, Daniels. Dennis Tracy, another old soldier, headed the largest precinct delegation, that from Cedar precinct, and manipulated the convention. Peters and Bollman were nominated by the help of Haire's delegation. Next came the nomination of sheriff.

The convention was held in the county court house, a wooden building about 18 by 26 feet in size. A small entry way was flanked on one side by a closet to hold county books and the other by a plank lined calaboose. I was an interested spectator standing in the hallway just behind Mr. Haire, the man who expected to receive the nomination for sheriff in return for his help in nominating the regular candidates for clerk and treasurer. The vote was on for sheriff and enough personal friends of Daniels helped by Tracy and other old soldiers, nominated Daniels. Immediately upon receiving the unexpected doublecross the defeated candidate, who was a large man and standing directly in front of me, fainted and fell over on me. I was much lighter in weight and had to call for help to drag him into the open air to revive him with a liberal splash of water.

The convention proved to be a Waterloo for the Antis although they started in confident with a convention majority, as they supposed. The sheriff nomination was a signal for a rapid retreat of the stalwart Antis to the drug store where several libations of drug store whiskey was required to revive their depressed spirits and make them good antimonopolists again.

But Dr. Lewis and his clansmen while outgeneraled at the county convention, were far from admitting defeat. The war went on vigorously. Neither side gave or asked mercy. At a later convention to choose delegates to a state convention and declare principles, Dr. Lewis managed to control the meeting. He erected a plank platform alongside his store building and got in the work planned, rapidly assisted by others and the oratory of Tom Wilkinson, an English labor agitator from a manufacturing city in England, held the audience spellbound. Tom was a well known champion of the farmers and a strong antimonopolist. The enemy orators vainly tried to get the ear of the assembled people but Dr. Lewis tore down the platform while they were trying to speak. Right there politics as worked in Indiana and Nebraska politics of the eighties clashed. An old man who hailed from Indiana where I did, was grieved. He was a rank republican of the strictest party sort. He was one of the few who did not object to being called an abolitionist in slavery times. As a rule, to be called an abolitionist was considered to be as great a disgrace up to 1863, as to be called a horse thief. The old man, seeing me a spectator, came to me and said sadly, "I don't like this kind of politics. I believe in the good old-fashioned way of fighting the democrats. This looks like brothers fighting."

So the fight went on in Nebraska for years. Van Wycke was elected to the United States Senate. Loran Clark was a leading republican in the state and a leading citizen of his home county. He was a public spirited man and did much for his home town but the Anti opposition called Clark and Peters bosses who made political slates. Peters held local county office but Clark asked little for himself. Once he was nominated for state treasurer but the

The national game. Batter up: pitcher in box: umpire on guard. It must not be presumed that the homesteaders of Nebraska never played. At least the younger generation believed the old adage that all work and no play makes Jack a dull boy. There were few dull Jacks or Jills during the sod house period. Country dances, social gatherings, picnics and other amusements were popular but base ball was pre-eminently the summer amusement. Probably a thousand games were played monthly as the country was settling. The period developed good base ball players as the sand lots of San Francisco and east side of Boston did.

Cherry Orchard Containing 500 Bearing Trees in Sod House Belt.

eloquence of Tom Wilkinson in the Anti state convention succeeded in having both democratic and antimonopoly conventions endorse the same candidate and Clark was defeated at the election.

Shell Creek precinct in the northeast corner of the county was populated by Norwegians who had followed a leader from Minnesota. They made a colony of about 100 voters but the colony grew by accretion. They were a very desirable class of citizens but because they understood very little English, they followed the first of their countrymen so that they might secure free homes among people who spoke their language and belonged to their Lutheran church. Before they could file on a homestead they had to declare their intention of becoming citizens and take out their first papers. They had to go before John Peters, county clerk, to make their application. The story was that after the first comers, others followed who could not understand English. Their friend took them before Peters who administered the oath in the usual mumbling tone, not a word of which was understood by the applicant. He asked his Norwegian friend to explain what Peters said. He explained, "It is like this; you are applying to become the citizen of a republic. John Peters is a republican. Therefore the meaning is that you must be a republican in politics." The election returns from that precinct for many years showed about 98 republican votes and three democrat votes furnished by three Danes who had a better knowledge of the language. Had Peters been a democrat they would probably have been told that they were being made citizens of a democracy and must be democrats.

In 1885 I bought the Albion Argus and the combined fusionists succeeded in electing part of the
county officers for several years but the national
and state vote was two-thirds republican. We had
to take turns and stand up and fight. One year the
contest was on straight party lines and the republican majority was 100 more than the total democratic vote. Still three of us were lucky enough to
be elected. The lowest man on the ticket was
County Judge Joseph Hamilton. A competent judge,
a good political worker and somewhat eccentric. At
that time each party provided its own election
tickets and stickers to paste over an opponent's
name so that a voter could vote his ticket and still
vote for a candidate on the other side. Late election night Judge Hamilton seemed hopelessly beat-
en, every voting precinct having been heard from
except the solidly republican Norwegian precinct,
and Hamilton was far behind. His defeat was con-
ceded.

Next day the Norwegian vote came in and instead
of the republican candidate for judge having 97
votes, Judge Hamilton had 97 votes which overcame
the majority against him and give him a lead of
12 votes in the county. It appeared that the Norwegian republican who came in to get the election
tickets for his precinct was a warm friend of Hamilton's and the two took the entire lot of republican
ballots and placed Hamilton stickers over his opponent's name as candidate for judge and this insured
him most of the Norwegian republican votes and
his election.

A story illustrated the feeling of the times. On
the southwest of Boone county Greeley county was

colonized by accretion by Irish who came from everywhere an Irishman should. They were princes in their own right and politics to them was second nature. They were as unanimously democrats and Catholics as the Norwegians were republicans and Lutherans. This story, vouched for by a district judge, but in my mind not conclusive, was that a Greeley Irishman laid at the point of death. His worldly affairs had been directed and the church had administered the last rites. He was still conscious and a friend asked if there was another last wish that he might express. He said there was. When he was prepared for burial he wanted to be buried in the northeastern corner of Boone county. As that would be among the Norwegian Lutheran republicans his friends in surprise asked the reason for such a strange request. He answered that there would be the last place the devil would look for a democrat Irishman.

The revolt against the republicans came in 1890 when the Peoples Independent Party, or Populist as it was called, received two-thirds of the votes in Boone county and about the same proportion in the state. In Boone, it was done partly by the good help of my paper. At the next county convention the populists pledged their candidates to show no courtesies to either old party. While they had appreciated my support they had desired a paper of their own and instead of being willing to buy my paper for what it was worth, undertook to freeze it out. They started a third paper backed by many well to do farmers in the county and eventually lost all they put into it.

The convention act was a signal for me to organize a county democratic party. The result was that the democrats cast only about 125 votes but instead of certain victory the populists failed to secure the best county offices. The office of sheriff showed a tie vote between an old Civil war veteran and a prosperous farmer. A tie was drawn and the republican got it. When I saw the good poker players helping make the draw, all doubts of the results left me. I felt certain that the republican would get it, which he did. I don't know how it was managed, but one said to me, "By gosh, we couldn't afford to take any risk." The defeated candidate was angry because I organized the democratic party and went to the printing office during my absence and stopped his paper and paid ten cents he owed. He informed the force that he was going to give me a beating the first time and place he met me. I came in while he was discoursing but he attempted no hostilities.

Pat Mathews was the democratic candidate for state representative in 1892. In Plum Creek precinct, two neighbors, Monte Wheeler, a democrat, and Jim Allen, a republican, worked in pairs. They were well-to-do farmers and engaged in local politics for amusement. As a rule, the republican leaders gave them a little money to use before election, and they always came to the county seat as soon as the polls closed and went home the next afternoon after I had lent them a little money to pay their local bills from the night before. At this election, closely contested between republicans and populists, the democrats hardly made a respectable third in votes secured. About midnight, Monte came to me and seemed worried about something. Pat Mathews had given him five dollars to look after Pat's vote in the precinct. Monte said that when he reported to Pat early in the evening, he told him that he had received two votes in the precinct. At midnight the report of the actual count came in and Pat did not have a single vote in the precinct. Monte said it left him in a dam embarrassing position. Monte had not voted for Pat himself.

The 1892 presidential and state election was hotly contested between the populists and I edited an exceedingly vigorous democratic paper, sparing neither populists or republicans. In spite of that I was re-elected county commissioner but it was solely on my business record. In a few years state and national fusion was brought about between the democrats and populists and I was picked on to send to the legislature. My business cares had increased and with probable victory confronting me, and a strong urge by my friends, I declined on the grounds that the democrats were the salt of the earth and that if they had either place it should be the senate. Besides I said that I would not consent to spend the winter among a hundred such rough necks as had usually comprised the lower house.

With fusion the democrats were allowed as many convention votes as the populists had. Our senatorial district was composed of Antelope, Boone and Greeley counties. I held several senatorial conventions with one Irishman from Greeley county. So in the state convention the apportionment would be 13 votes for our county. Thirteen populist delegates went to their state convention and I alone went to the democratic state convention, carrying 13 votes. I became postmaster at Albion in April, 1894, and resigned the office of county commissioner.

I was in the democratic state convention at Lincoln in 1895 when W. J. Bryan, a young democratic congressman, asked the convention to "sit down on Grover," which they refused to do. He had the Lincoln delegation but the big Omaha delegation prevented the humiliating of a democratic president. In 1896 Bryan spent several weeks before the state convention in Omaha and succeeded in capturing the Omaha delegation. As county seat postmaster I was called on to bring to the convention an administration delegation and I reported with a carefully selected assortment of postmasters and Cleveland democrats. But Bryan had a majority in the convention and Satan was running loose. Bryan's plan was to secure fusion with the populists and endorse all of their state candidates, save only the democratic candidate for attorney general, just enough to bind the two parties in fusion. After much confusion Bryan took the platform and announced that he was about to take a step that his friends advised would bring his political death. That if it was so, so be it. His blood would be on his own head. He moved to place in nomination for governor on the democratic ticket, Silas Holcomb, the nominee of the populists. He followed by moving the endorsement of the populist lieutenant governor. The confusion became so great that no further convention work was possible for some time. The administration delegates mostly bolted the convention, and someone held an adjourned convention and elected delegates to the national convention, soon to be held in Chicago. As soon as the convention quieted, it proceeded to endorse the populist state officers according to the slate, and elect a full set of delegates hand picked by Bryan to attend the national convention. The delegates elected were agreeable to Bryan's paramount issue of free coinage of silver at the ratio of 16 to 1. The adjourned convention sent a delegation of gold democrats to the national convention who were actually seated till displaced by the committee on credentials.

I kept my delegation in the convention. The endorsement of the populist candidates was distasteful to us but Bryan had secured control of the convention honestly. As an example of the sentiment, I heard the chairman of a delegation whipping a dissatisfied delegate into line with the following argument. "You know blank well that you could not have been on this delegation had we objected. You should know that this is a Bryan convention. If Bryan says that Holcomb, the populist nominee for governor, is to be endorsed, it is to be done. If he says to endorse the republican candidate for governor, the endorsement will be made. This is a Bryan convention. You had better climb into the band-wagon."

The result of the national convention is well known. Bryan made his celebrated crown of thorns and cross of gold speech and was nominated and might have been elected President had not the gold democrats bolted the ticket. At home, the gold or administration democrats balked at free silver at first but after trying it, as one said, "It was not so bad to take after all."

The financial panic of 1893 and the resulting low prices for farm produce and the actual loss of a crop in 1894 brought on a political revolt among the farmers of the western states. As usual, in sudden movements of the people, barnacles joined them to benefit themselves. They killed the populist ship of state and dispersed its members to their former parties. But among populists were some wonderful politicians. They would gather the people for hundreds of miles around at a central meeting place for an ox roast and to listen to many speeches. Doc Bixby, of the Nebraska State Journal, condensed what he called their platform of procedure, in a four line virile poem—

"I cannot sing the old songs,
My heart is full of woe,
But I can howl calamity
From hell to Broken Bow."

The farmers were greatly displeased with the editorial utterances of the Lincoln Journal, one of the leading republican daily papers in the state. The Journal bluntly asserted that the farmers would be as much out of place in the administrative offices of the state as hogs in a parlor. It was believed by many that the populists elected their entire state ticket in 1890 and were counted out of the places by a conspiracy of the two old parties that gave the governorship to the democratic candidate, James Boyd, and the other state offices to the republican candidates.

At the meeting of the joint session of the legislature January 7, 1891, the proceedings were very confusing and the joint session turned into a howling, excited mob. The populists were not accus-

tomed to parliamentary usage. They had elected
Samuel Elder speaker of the house, and apparently
it was his right to preside. The joint session was
held for canvassing the state votes and declaring
the elected state officers. As the populists designed
declaring that John Powers, their candidate, was
elected governer and all their state candidates to
their respective places, the control of the joint session was important. Lieutenant Governor Meikeljohn invaded the joint session and took a place in
front of Speaker Elder and usurped his place. He
did it with such brazen assurance that the populists,
in their inexperience, did not know what to do. The
doors were closed and Speaker Elder sent a request
to Governor Thayer for a military guard to preserve order and save destruction of property, and
it was provided.

Eventually adjournment was taken and canvassing the contested votes and hearing the contests,
was left to a committee and the result was finally
declared that James Boyd, democrat, was elected
governor and the entire republican state executive
officers were elected to their respective places. Many
people believed that had the populists had experience, and Speaker Elder been forceful and strong,
the result would have been different.

The sentiment among the farmers of the state
was that they had been betrayed by their rulers and
law makers. Especially did they blame the republican congressmen for making hard times and making money scarce. As county commissioner, I had
nine men at work one day with their teams grading a hilly road. All were farmers who worked to
earn a little ready cash. Seven of them were out-

spoken populists. One was indifferent. One lone
man was a republican. The seven made life a burden for the lone republican with their charges that
the republican congressman, Dorsey, was to blame
for the low prices of farm products and the shortage of money. Finally Tommy Roach, the indifferent
man, who was an elderly Irishman of democratic
leanings, took up for the oppressed republican fellow workman and the reviled congressman by
saying, "Oh, by hell I shall vote for Dorsey because
he is the mon who made pigs cheap when I wanted
to buy."

I still edited my paper. The populist farmers
were personally friendly to me and grieved that I
did not fully endorse their propaganda. It happened that the man whom I had defeated for office
as a republican, turned populist with the crowd. He
was a unique character and endured criticism well.
He had assisted in his own defeat by spending most
of his district share of the county road-money to
make a four mile air line wagon road as he called
it, through the hilliest part of the county, to his
farm. The road was very unpopular. Some of my
farmer friends asked me to stop criticising this man,
but I had not fully obeyed. Mentioning the man
editorially I said that it was reported that Joe
Anderson in going home over his county airline
had broken the neckyoke to his buggy by the end
of the tongue striking the road while going up one
of the steep hills. One Saturday afternoon returning
from the country, I was stopped by one of my con-
stitutents, a German farmer, slightly Volsteadized,
who called me to halt and administered the following
reprimand. "Say," he said, "I thought I told you to

let up on old Choe but here you are giving him hell
and tamnation again. Of course you know, you are
all right, but you are just a little too tam fresh."

The populists came and were active and disap-
peared. There was good reason for their coming
and perhaps the time had arrived for their going.
Among those militant farmers were many men of
ability and lawyers coming from town to talk them
out of their alleged fallacies, and to get them to
return to the old party fold, were many times
humiliated. Once a well known mid-Nebraska lawyer went out to a country school house to make a
republican speech. One of the audience gave a
curtain-riser talk. He said that the year before he
was a stalwart republican himself, but since then
his eyes had been opened. That he went out with
the lawyer who was to speak to them, to help him
hold a republican meeting. Examination of the
lawyer's buggy uncovered a bottle of whisky which
he had appropriated and later used to drench a mule.
The lawyer met the occasion by asserting that he
did not come that night to make a republican speech
or any other speech, but had been for a year search-
ing for the man who stole and drank his whisky,
and by the "great horn-spoon" he had found him.

Calling republican leaders, bosses and slate
makers, did not please them. Democrat leaders
denied that anyone except republicans endured
party bosses or made political slates. Once, before
populist times, a worthy Irishman visited me just
before convention time for election of county officers, and asked me to put him onto the slate so
he could work understandingly. I answered, "My
dear sir, the democrats have no slates. They have

no bosses as the republicans have. Anyone you may think is a boss is simply a common democrat, working for the people as a servant, to carry out their wishes. They fix up no slates, but leave it for the people in convention assembled to choose their public servants." The Irishman was interested, but insisted, "Yes, but I could work more understandingly if yez would put me onto the slate."

The pioneer melting pot that strove to part the political royal metal from the dress ceased to function after 1897. Out of it all came the cosmopolitan Nebraska representative featuring a great and prosperous state.

The political conventions of later times did not harmonize with the political conventions of Jefferson, Hamilton, Lincoln, Cleveland and Roosevelt. I am reminded of a county convention that happened in 1912 while I was an interested and amused bystander.

At that time I was publishing the Albion Argus and editing it as my part of the work. My foreman was a young man who had attained the altitude of six feet three and latitude of about ten inches. He went by the name of "Slim" Davis. "Slim" was captain of the local National Guard company and his main theme was the prospect of getting into war with Mexico where he could slake his thirst for martial gore. I warned him that his altitude would expose him to the shots of the "greasers" because they would get him above the mesquite trees, so generous had nature dealt with him in his altitude. He claimed that his hope was to offset the risk by windage because of his narrow latitude.

"Slim" favored a president who doted on war, hence was friendly to "Teddy," but in an unguarded moment he went to the republican county convention and returned to his job elated because he had been elected chairman of the republican county central committee. That put him in line with the regular republican machine and he was obliged to support Taft. He said that if I had done my part I would have secured the chairmanship of the democrats, and Poynter, formerly connected with the Argus, would be chairman of the half dozen populists who kept up the populist organization. I was shocked and remonstrated with him for accepting the chairmanship of a party known to be antagonistic to the settled policy of the paper he was working for, but he held on to the position.

1912 broke with the air full of "Bull Moose Movements," "Teddy," "Progressives" and "Old Guard" contentions. "Teddy" had come home from Africa loaded down with lion tails and full of fight for the "Progressive" republicans and it took strong in our county. The honorable chairman of the republican county central committee was driven into close quarters. He called the county convention to meet after the caucuses, and in due time the reports began to flock in. His position compelled him to be a machine politician and follow Taft. Precinct after precinct reported to him "so many" Bull Moose delegates; "so many" Teddy; "so many" Progressive, just as the name happened to remind them, but every precinct delegation in the county was for the insurgents and not one for the Taft administration.

In his quandary "Slim" appealed to me to know what he could do. I told him that when the delegates gathered that the only course open was to call them to order and take his coat and hat and get out. There were many standpat republicans who urged him to stay by the ship. They would support the Brimstone Majesty before they would Teddy. I will not deny that as a loyal employe he asked further advice of me. In order to see that the plan was carried out right I concluded to forego attending the democrat convention and take a seat in the center of the district court room and learn the ways the republicans had of conducting things at a convention where the party was having a bully fight.

In due time the delegates gathered and seated themselves in an orderly way and visited and counseled with each other in a very friendly manner. They were all dandy fine fellows and my personal friends. "Slim," the honorable county chairman, seated himself within the bar in a very dignified way in keeping with the responsibility of his position. Finally he arose and called time on the unsuspecting delegates and made the following appropriate address:

"Gentlemen: "The mightiest effort ever made by mankind for material advancement, and in the interests of humanity that the world ever witnessed, was made by these United States of America under the benign and wise management of the republican party. Little progress was made till the republican party took charge of the ship of state and directed the destiny of our country. The republican party gave to the country that mighty statesman, the immortal Lincoln. It gave the greatest war hero of

all time, General Grant. It gave us Logan and Gar-
field and William Howard Taft. It gave freely of
multitudes of mighty men of great ability who were
self sacrificing and loyal. The Stars sang in chorus
at the birth of the republican party and its history
has been glorious.

"In progress in the arts and sciences the world
marvels at what the republican party freely brought
to the people. In industries, unequalled and un-
rivalled; in its administration of the government it
has surpassed the wisdom of Solomon; to the republican party the world is indebted for the telegraph,
the telephone, electric inventions. Under the fos-
tering care of the republican party the prairies of
the west, with their untold wealth hidden in the rich
soil, were developed. The republican party gave
homesteads to poor but industrious farmers for the
price of living on the land a short period. All
advance is due the Grand Old Party as conducted by
its wonderfully active and able public men, not the
least of whom is William Howard Taft.

"The republican party saved the union of the
states and put down the rebellion of the south.
Providence and humanity perched on its banner
and it prevailed. It liberated 3,000,000 colored
people held in bondage against their will. It gave
them the right to vote. The former slaves cry the
glory of the party that made them free men and
free women.

"In education all advance is due the republican
party. They it was who placed red school houses
in all the hollows and on all hill tops. They gave
education to the young people and now all those who
run may read. They reduced the toil of the hard

working farmer by inventing harvesting machinery
and labor saving farm implements to the end that
his toil was lessened, his hours of labor shortened
and he enjoyed the thrill of being a citizen of a
republic, whose boast exceeded that of the Roman,
who said that to be a citizen of Rome was greater
than to be a king. To the republican party of
America be all praise and all glory for its accomplishments and its great and self-sacrificing men
and women.

"But gentlemen: What do I see before me? My
eyes do not deceive me, nor my ears fail me, nor
does my sense of understanding with which nature
endowed me fail to sustain me in this critical sit-
uation. I see a gathering of men who are not republicans who would hold a convention in the name
of the Grand Old Party of Lincoln and Grant. They
would betray the party brought into being by the
sainted Lincoln and continued to the present by
William Howard Taft, into the hands of traitors
who would disrupt the party that has done so much
for our nation, our people and for civilization. Gentlemen: I cannot, I will not stultify myself and betray the people by dignifying this gathering by calling it to order as a republican convention. I will
accordingly retire from the room until such time as
a gathering of republicans may assemble to accom-
plish the will of the nation, by assembling as republicans, instead of counterfeits who call themselves "Progressives," "Bull Moosers" or "Teddy-
ites" but who work for the injury of the republican
party, and the downfall of our nation."

As he proceeded I watched the delegates, and was
astonished that they did not arise and put "Slim"

out of doors. Apparently the affair came on so un-
expectedly that their minds were benumbed and did
not work in unison. They looked crushed and in-
credulous. At the close of his address the chairman
left the presiding officer's chair and in the most
thoughtless and unwise way came down into the
middle of the room and took a seat close to me. All
of those miserable delegates had been looking toward me already and one of my close personal
friends, withal a stanch republican, came and told
me that it was a "dumb mean trick." The most
active delegates began to warm up and try to get
"Slim" to call them to order and told him just what
I had warned him would be his fate, that he could
then take his coat and go home. He came back at
them by telling them that if they could satisfy him
that they were republicans, and would support the
republican candidates, that he would call them to
order. One man declared that it had come to a
pretty pass when a young man could question the
republicanism of men who were voters before he
was born. All the time orators were talking to the
audience and to the world at large expounding on
the orneryness of the chairman, all the time talking,
but all the time looking right at me, much to my
embarrassment.

"Slim's" charges questioning their republicanism
cut deep but finally somebody nominated a chairman
and the convention settled down to work without
having been assembled by the regular county chairman whose term of office had expired on the moment, day and date herein mentioned.

Much excitement prevailed on the street. One
lawyer improvised on the story of Jacob and Esau

and asserted that it was the voice of "Slim" Davis but the hand of "Doc" Barnes directed the whole proceedings. Another "Bull Mooser" scolded vehemently and asserted that things had come to a helluva pass when the right to discipline their own leaders was interfered with by the measly democrats.

However, a well known stalwart Taft man claimed that a part of the credit for the speech and procedure was due him because three drinks of his whiskey had found lodgment under "Slim's" vest.

That night the speech was rehearsed many times by "Slim" in his zeal to keep control of the country from the despised Bull Moose party. He was invited to attend the "Rump" administration convention at Lincoln although the county was unanimous for "Teddy," but I was obliged to assert my chairmanship of the printing office and order the doughty captain to go on guard duty among the quads and nonpareil shooting sticks of the office.

CHAPTER XIV

Character Sketches

"Laugh and the world laughs with you;
Weep and you weep alone.
For the sad old earth must borrow its mirth,
But has troubles enough of its own."
—*Wilcox*.

NEBRASKA state, during its formative period, had many interesting characters. As a rule they were above the average in intelligence and were positive in their pronouncements. T h e i r peculiarities ranged from natural or acquired drolleries to the keenest kind of wit. Among them it is but fair to mention Edgar Howard, who came to Nebraska in 1882, and made his presence known without delay. At the time these reminiscences were written he had been elected to his fourth term as congressman from the Third Nebraska district.

Mr. Howard claimed to descend from the Quakers of New England and that he retained their ways. He looked the part of a Quaker with his supersolemn countenance and long hair, and for the most part wearing a broad-brimmed hat, if he wore any hat at all. But he did not always act like a Quaker. Quakers were supposed to speak only when moved by the spirit but the spirit labored with Edgar and moved him to speak almost any time. His ability to build up a word picture was unsurpassed and his vocabulary abundant.

Mr. Howard divided his time between writing editorials for his paper and serving his political party

in conventions and the councils of his party. He
served as county judge of a county near Omaha, was
sent to the state senate once, defeated for congress
near Omaha once, and then moved to Columbus
about 90 miles west of Omaha and threw in with
the most reliable democratic county in Nebraska.
The year Nebraska voted for constitutional prohibition he was elected lieutenant governor. He ad-
vocated prohibition but did not look darkly on people who did not practice prohibition, and even had
a kindly feeling toward John Barleycorn himself,
alleging that he did not hold that opinion or so act
with the intent of harming his fellow man.

During the W. J. Bryan period, fusion between
the populist, democrat and free silver republican
parties was sought and accomplished in order to defeat the republican state and local candidates.
Bryan, although a democrat always favored giving
nearly all the places to the populist candidates to
keep their hearts right. In one of these old time
state conventions, where candidates for all state offices were to be nominated, Bryan proposed to let
the tail wag the dog by giving the governorship and
most of the state offices to the populists. He reserved national office for himself. Mr. Howard led
the delegation from Columbus and nearly spilt the
beans by insisting that the democrats nominate one
of their party as candidate for governor, well knowing that the slate was made up to nominate a populist.

The spirit of Jackson and Jefferson was troubled
and looked disapprovingly on the rebellion of Mr.
Howard to the well known orders of W. J. Bryan.
The spirit of Jefferson and Jackson was moved

mightily and Mr. Howard was beset from all sides
to withdraw his objections and lead his big delegation into the camp of the silver tongued orator, and
use the password. Finally it was agreed that Mr.
Howard should have all the time he wanted to explain why his county objected to giving the populists the governorship and Judge W. H. Thompson
should have 20 minutes in which to answer him.
Little did they know that they were giving the advantage to a man, who in the future, would become
one of the most adroit and gifted speakers in the
state.

Edgar began in his slow, deliberate way, with his
usual Quaker drawl, to explain his position. He
said, "You people do not understand what it is to
live in the only democratic stronghold in the state.
To be sent to the state convention to nominate a
democrat for governor, and then have to take a
night train for home, go up a dark street, sneak up
a back alley and crawl into your yard through the
dog hole in the fence, for fear you will meet a
democrat constituent who will ask you, 'Did you
vote for a democrat for governor just once,'" Every
one, including Judge Thompson, was an intent list-
ener, when Edgar broke suddenly and announced,
"But I love my country more than I do the republican governor and I will give in." A tremendous
ovation followed.

Once he desired to be accepted as the democratic
candidate for congress while the district was represented by a republican. He did some gum-shoe work
in the district to see what his chances for the nomi-
nations were. He visited me and stated his case
and desires. He said, "I told the boys I did not

know why I should ask the voters of the Third district to do me this great honor. Nor could I say why my own party owed it to me to send me to congress, but I did say to the boys that if they would send me to Washington to represent them, I would agree to have as good a time as any one they could send." In time he did become congressman and established a reputation as one of the best story-tellers and most interesting short speech-makers in congress, and he served his constituents well, too.

J. E. Needham was for a long time the leading hotel keeper in his part of the state. He was one of the narrowest and most uncompromising republicans to be found anywhere. He was a pure New England yankee and went by the name of "Yank." At one time the republican state officers scandalized the state by their conduct. "Yank" expressed his opinion that there was the blankest set of robbers and thieves in office at the state house ever seen. Any party that kept such people in office would, sooner or later, be beaten and dam 'em they ought to be. As an afterthought he added, "But we must vote for them just the same. We should vote the ticket even if there is a yellow dog on it."

One of the leading lawyers of the state, W. V. Allen of Madison, was elected United States senator by the populists. Soon after his election Mr. Allen attended court in "Yank's" town and was a guest at his hotel. To show courtesy, Mr. Needham hired the best livery rig available at the time which was a canopy top, two-seated buggy, to take the senator on an inspection trip about town. He apologized for the opulence of the rig by saying that he should have got a lumbuh wagon to take a Fa'muh's Alliance senatuh on a ride.

When Cleveland retired from office after his first term so great a surplus was left in the U. S. Treasury that it scandalized the country. "Yank" said, "God help the su'plus when we get hold of it." Toward the close of Cleveland's second term when times were hard and I was serving as a Cleveland postmaster, "Yank" would announce in the lobby of the office that good times and plenty of work would soon be enjoyed because the republicans would be in power. "Wait so many months and week and days and hours and all will be well," was his constant admonition. W. J. Bryan was expected to visit the town and hold a meeting during the 1896 campaign and I induced the merchants to decorate in his honor. "Yank" also decorated his hotel. I asked for an explanation and he responded that he had worked pretty hard and desired a rest so he temporarily honored Bryan as work was always scarce under "dimmycratic" leadership.

Harness racing on the fair ground track between roadster horses was popular. "Yank" and a young barber bought a driving horse that could make a mile in 3:20 when his splints and spavins did not cause him to hitch and break by their tenderness. Advice was given them as to the care of a race horse. The barber was induced to give a light oat feed and very little hay and only blanket "Dexter's" head after a "work out." "Yank" insisted that an animal called on to do hard work should be fed on good hay and a big feed of corn to give him strength. The blanket should go all over the horse. At length a trial of speed was arranged between another owner who had a 3:40 horse and a small bet on the result was posted. The other party managed to get

"Dexter" to have a good drink of water and heavy feed of hay and grain to give him strength for the ordeal. Another party induced the owners to use a strong liniment on "Dexter's" curbs and splints to soothe him for the race. The liniment made the legs sore and made the horse break horribly and the big feed incapacitated him so much that the slower horse beat him.

A goodly sized colony of Irish had gathered by accretion, most of them coming from the same neighborhood in Wisconsin. There was one man among them who was called old. He was born in Ireland and had had no opportunity to secure an education. He had on intrepid spirit and showed it by breaking away and going to the country that welcomed people of his courage and gave them a man's chance. He had the courage and disposition to resent injuries, typical of his class. He accumulated property and gave his children all the education possible and they in turn sent their own children higher up the ladder. He was made the subject of many jokes, respectfully perpetrated, but in the spirit of humor.

The Catholics had no house of worship and most of the Irish belonged to the Catholic Church. Soon they began to plan for a church building in the nearby town. A building committee led by the pastor, planned for a wooden church building. Two of the church members were casually sitting and talking one afternoon when they saw their old friend approaching. Pretending to not see him they engaged in earnest conversation, all intended for his ear. One said, "The building committee is making some progress with the church, and have got some cash subscriptions, some labor subscriptions to do common work or hauling material, and are probably doing the best they can, but I think it is a dom poor idea to shingle the church wid paper shingles."

"And is it paper shingles the rogues are going to put on our church. Oim not going to church and have a rain storm come up and the dirty rain water trickling down through me hair."

"Sure they are going to use paper shingles because they are cheap and there comes now the dirty traveling man who is going to sell the shingles to the committee." The traveling man referred to had just come in on the train and was ignorant of what they charged him with, and shingles was not his line.

The old man had been intently listening as was planned. He could stand it no longer and came to the rescue in a militant way. "Bedad," he said, "Oill not stand for thot." He met the innocent traveling salesman and cursed him for trying to over reach the church committee by selling them paper to roof the building with and warned him to turn back and abandon his evil purpose and leave town if he would preserve his safety.

Village office appointments went by political party favor. Once when the old man's son and myself had been elected members of the village board, and I was to be chairman of the board with appointing power, and could nominate the appointive officials, subject to confirmation by the board, the old man approached me while I was talking with parties on the street. He addressed me excitedly saying, "I would like to spake a word wid yez in private." I followed him but we had hardly gone twenty feet when he spoke in a voice easily heard a block and said, "The democrats be having a majority on the town board and their friends should now come into their own. I want to be appointed marshal and street commissioner." I answered him that his son and myself were democrats assuredly, but the other three were republicans. He named Sam Hetzler, one of the three saying that Sam was a democrat. I told the old man that Hetzler was one of the firmest republicans in town. Evidently his Irish friends had been stringing him. He seemed disappointed but answered bravely, "Then he lies most damnedly."

The county had one colored citizen. The old negro had served as a soldier in a colored detachment during the Civil war. He did not know how old he was but had been a house slave before the war and was honest and faithful. The G. A. R. always made him color bearer on Decoration Day. Old Bill would obey orders to the letter. During one of the county fairs I had engaged Bill as policeman on the grounds. The barb-wire fence was little help to repel invaders who desired to avoid buying a ticket, and Bill was instructed to keep a look out for such intruders and arrest them and take them to the ticket office and make them buy a ticket. The old

Irish man was on the ground and went outside through the fence for something and Bill saw him when he returned and promptly arrested him. Bill's orders were to arrest anyone coming in through the fence but he had no orders to arrest those going out. It was interesting to see the result. Here was a fighting Irishman being compelled to obey a "dirty black nagur" and being taken under duress across the grounds in view of his friends, all the while fighting back and arguing loudly in fluent brogue about the indignity shown an American citizen. All the time the secret applause of the second generation of Irish was freely indulged in.

While there was not a drunkard among the entire lot one of them said that every Irishman when he goes to a new town wants a drink of whiskey, why he did not know. One of the colonists would, at long intervals, get to drinking in town and would perhaps stay over night, when some one would send him home and administer a reprimand. This man had malarial attacks before coming to Nebraska. An old grocery merchant had such a solemn visage that it attracted attention of the Irish. When this Irishman was found in town one morning, having stayed all night and got a drop too much, he was admonished by an influential friend. He answered, "I came to town with the best of intentions and intended to return home about me business, but I got a look at Holly, (the grocer mentioned) and it brought on a touch of the agy and I took a drop to throw off the chill and some how was not able to stop and here I am in my disgrace."

Another one had lost an arm under tragic conditions. Returning home late one December night when the weather was snappy cold and a bright starlight sky, he unhitched his team of nervous mules and while watering them at the trough the big snap on the end of the strap that held up the neckyoke became fastened in his clothing and before he could detach it the mule took fright and ran away, dragging him over the frozen ground back and forth through a corn field, striking, kicking and biting in a frenzy to get rid of the load that frightened him. When at last the man fell loose, his arm was broken and so badly bitten that it had to be amputated.

This man was judged by traveling men to have lost his arm during the Civil war and was respected accordingly. A sympathetic gathering of traveling men met him on the platform while awaiting for a train and asked him about the loss of the arm, and he responded that he lost it at Antietam. When asked if he received a good pension he said "Not a darn cent." Neither democrats or republicans would help him. They were all ingrates. A friend of this man who knew him in Wisconsin was a candidate for county treasurer. He was also grain buyer at an elevator. He was grieved to hear that his old friend had said that he would not vote for him or any man who would take 35 pounds for a bushel of oats. The candidate asked him if he said those things. He said he did. When pressed to show where or when the candidate had ever taken such weights he said he never knew of such an instance but only said he would vote for no man who did take 35 pounds of oats for a bushel.

An old Kentuckian was an early day homesteader and for years the only auctioneer for miles around. He was scrupulously careful to pay his obligations promptly and strong for the old Kentucky church doctrine of predestination, foreordination and justification. He was also an unwavering democrat. He refused to vote for his own son who was a candidate for county commissioner on the republican ticket. He admitted that his son would make a competent official but said he had raised him better than to train with "them whelps."

It was reported of him while acting as an early day constable that he arrested a man charged with fighting, and collected his fee from the man on the spot. The man was found guilty in justice court and fined. Then the court followed the usual custom of remitting all costs because it was known that settlers were needy. The constable had foreseen this. Another time he was charged with taking up a collection of a dollar each to buy a man an overcoat that he said was badly needed. He took the money and bought himself a coat. When charged with duplicity, he answered that he needed the coat all right but they all could have their money back if they wanted it. Another time he returned from a visit to Kentucky, and while he did not use whiskey himself, he brought a small bottle of old choice Kentucky whiskey with him. He attended a farm sale and in a mysterious way invited an old Irish acquaintance to go behind a corn crib with him. There he displayed the whiskey and removing the cork told the Irishman to smell of it. Of course the smell was tantalizing and a drink was expected. The Irishman was rebuked by being told that it was too precious to waste on a common Irishman.

Typical of Irish humor it was reported of Greeley county that a state game warden learning of a violation of game laws by a Greeley county farmer came in on a train and took a team and brought the offender to town and held him over night to hale into the justice court next morning. The ride being chilly the game warden kindly gave his prisoner a drink of whiskey from the bottle he carried. Next morning he appeared at the justice court and with great assurance demanded that the violator of the game law be brought to trial so he could take the train out of town. Here the majesty of the law was invoked.

The justice severely informed him that there was a far more important matter and greater infringement of law that took precedence over the simple fact of a farmer shooting a prairie chicken, and it must be attended to first. A serious infraction of the liquor laws had been perpetrated. That the warden was charged with giving away liquor and the complaint must be heard before the less important cases had attention. There could be but one ending and the game warden was glad to get out of town without pressing the charge of shooting a prairie chicken.

In the country lived a family consisting of the wife and mother who was one of those pugnacious, if not vicious Irish women, who will fight a stack of wild cats any time. There were two grown sons who inherited their mother's disposition and a husband and father who had been taught his place. The family were land renters and had gotten into debt for farm equipment that they failed to pay for. The implement dealer who sold the equipment, the traveling salesman, the collector, the lawyer, all tried to make adjustments but were repelled with threats of violence, and failed to secure settlement. Greeley had a well beloved sheriff, one of the finest, biggest hearted men in the state. His purse was always open to relieve suffering and while a devout Catholic and supported his own church well, he helped all manner of other churches within forty miles. He was sent out to replevin a grain-binder that the family would neither settle for nor surrender. The report of the visit was told by the sheriff's admirers and the way he managed it was made to reflect well upon his good judgment.

It was a fine morning when Sheriff Flannagan drove up to the O'Flaharty home. The door opened and the militant head of the household appeared. The sheriff remarked "Good morning to yez, Mrs. O'Flaharty." "The top of the morning to yez Mr. Flannagan," answered the lady. "What are yez afther wanting, Mr. Flannagan?" "I am afther wanting that binder, Mrs. O'Flaharty." "Wait a moment, Mr. Flannagan," she said and went inside the house and returned with a double-barreled shotgun and got the drop on the sheriff. "What are yez afther wanting, Mr. Flannagan?" "I am afther wanting to go home" was the tactful answer. And the binder stayed on the farm.

Tim Mahoney was a prominent and successful business man. He was also a democrat without blemish and never varied even to become a fusionist or populist. Once both democrat and populist delegates met from the three counties to agree upon a fusion candidate for state senator. Antelope county being strong for populism and less so for democracy, sent a full delegation of populists to the convention and a lone delegate to represent the democrats. Greeley did the opposite thing and a full democrat delegation appeared with Mr. Mahoney an ex-officio delegate. He was introduced to the populist delegates from Antelope county and absent mindedly shook their hands. Then he was named to the democrat delegate from that county and brightened visibly. "Put it there partner," he said offering his hand. "A democrat hand savors of good fellowship, of good rich warm blood and flesh and of good will and good government. But taking these 'pops' by the hand is like taking hold of a greased pig's back, it gets your hand dirty and just slips off."

Mahoney was known as a state wide character. A leading state democrat told me he introduced Mahoney to a prominent citizen of Lincoln who was a talkative republican. He began to talk and Mr. Mahoney listened without interposing a word until the Lincoln man stopped for breath. Then Mahoney turned coolly to the man who had introduced him and remarked, "The dam thing can speak, it can articulate." This same man cursed a state senator soundly for the arrogance of a common pop introducing two democratic gentlemen to each other. That if there was a democrat in Nebraska it was Doc Barns. Soon after I declined to take a drink with him and he surveyed me carefully and expressed the fear that I had become a dam pop.

The enthusiastic Irish of Nebraska fairly worshipped W. J. Bryan, especially during the period of his greatest popularity, immediately after the 1896 presidential campaign. To them the young, eloquent, Mr. Bryan was almost a god. It was reported of an elderly Irishman that he was a great admirer of "The little Irish Orator," but he had been in ill health and confined to his bed for nearly a year and a half waiting for the summons to come to call him for his final departure. A delegation of Irishmen were escorting Bryan from the town where he had spoken last, to their home town where Bryan was expected to draw the curtain from the blarney stone for the benefit of home folks. Passing the farm house where his invalid admirer was lying on a bed of pain, Mr. Bryan was informed of the condition of his fellow democrat who was so much disappointed that he could not go out to meet him and hear him speak. Mr. Bryan requested that they might stop and let him meet the sick man. He made the visit and talked a few minutes with his admirer, who was greatly comforted by the old, old story of Jeffersonianism. His Irish friends are responsible for the story that the sick man was so nearly restored to health by Mr. Bryan doing him the honor of making him a personal call, that he arose, dressed himself, and enjoyed fair health for the next year and a half, so great was the appeal of the magnetic commoner to him.

So one could go on at great lengths. The makers of the state possessed humor as well as industry and perseverance. They were great admirers of their daily newspaper and editors and reporters. Richard L. Metcalf, long time reporter for the Omaha World-Herald, later its editor and a stanch supporter of W. J. Bryan, and competent to fill any place in the gift of the people, those early characters almost idolized.

An eccentric grass widower named Hans Schneider lived near us on his homestead. He claimed that Switzerland was his place of nativity but he was usually classed as a German. His wife refused to follow him from St. Louis to a sod house on the wild prairie, so he divorced her and lived alone. He professed to understand three languages and found them of great help to discipline or reprimand his ox team and was able to curse them in all three languages. His cooking and kitchen habits were very elementary and crude. When employed far from his home, he sometimes prepared a sandwich for his noon day lunch by placing thin slices of uncooked salt pork between two slices of bread. He lost no hogs during the epidemic of hog cholera although it was fatal to most farm herds. He said his remedy would be, in case that his hogs became infected, to climb into the pen with a butcher knife and soon have them in the pork barrel for his own table.

I asked Hans why he lived so like a hog himself and suggested that he find a good strong German girl somewhere and make her his wife. He informed me that such a thought was in his mind. A prosperous family that farmed on a large scale lived near by and they had a splendid young German girl working for them. One Sunday Hans was seen driving in the direction of the abiding place of the aforesaid young girl in his farm wagon accompanied by the Sunday school superintendent, who was also a justice of the peace and legally qualified for performing marriage ceremonies. It developed that Hans was taking the justice of the peace with him to marry him to the girl on the farm. He had not thought it necessary to advise the girl of the unexpected event. He admitted later that he once told her he was going to marry her some time but she passed over the statement lightly. On arrival at the home they found that the girl had gone with the family to church and the surprise was great to find that a wedding had been planned for the girl during her absence. Hans was soon made to know that the course of true love sometimes finds the road rough and he was indignantly repulsed for his caveman way of wooing a bride. A more leisurely courtship extending about a year followed and a wedding succeeded by a prosperous home and family added to the social life of the neighborhood.

Amidst their privations and hardships the pioneers had their diversions. The signs of age had not appeared on many of them and they still felt the joy of life springing up in their hearts. W. A. Poynter, a farmer living near by was elected governor of the state by a fusion of democrats, populists and free silver republicans. An elderly Irishman hearing that I might have influence with the governor sought me with the information that he wanted to be appointed to an office. He said, "We are now victorious and I hear that the democrats do be afther having a third part of the offices and I have always been a democrat and now want an office." I explained that there were at least thirty applicants for each office and the procedure was to choose the office he aspired to and get influential people to endorse him for the place and present it to the governor. I asked him what office he had in mind that he wanted. His response was prompt, "How the hell should I know. I want something where the pay is big and the work light and aisy." He then insisted that I write his petition for an office. I wrote it with an effort to start and go in a circle and return to the place of beginning without saying anything. He asked me to endorse him first but I assured him that it would be inconsistent for me to sign his petition because I had written it. I advised that he go to the court house and get the populist county officers to endorse him. This he did, but secured no office.

CHAPTER XV

Ox-Team Freighting

"The daily routine of a bull whacker's life on the trail, while a hard one, was not all clouds. Each day's experiences would make an interesting chapter if written. We would be awakened by the night riders at about 3:30 A. M. with the call, "Cattle in the corral." This meant for all to roll out and the night riders to turn in. The bull whackers in camp when there were no wheels to fix, no tires to tighten, boxes to wedge, oxen to shoe, or clothes to wash or mend, could sleep, play cards, write letters or tell stories."—*Bratt.*

 I enjoyed a personal acquaintance with Edward Hall, a prosperous cattle man whose ranch was located on Beaver Creek, in northwestern Boone county, on the sand hill cattle ranges. We were associate members of the county board of commissioners of Boone county for three years. He was a strong man, physically and mentally, and had secured a very practical business education by contact with business men, while train boss of freighting trains between Nebraska City and the mountains, as far west as Salt Lake City. He was a well poised man and was a fine judge of human nature but had very little book education. It goes without saying that he made an excellent county commissioner and could grasp some of the problems that we were confronted with better than had he been favored with a college education. And he was what people called, "Absolutely straight."

At the time Mr. Hall took service with one of the great freighting companies, the Missouri river starting place across the plains was at Nebraska City. It was a typical frontier town and full of life

and activity. It was also a pretty tough place where
everything was wide open. Saloons, gambling
houses, dance halls and all manner of rough amusements were there to entice the wages from the in-
coming and outgoing "bull whackers," as the drivers of the ox teams were called. Anyone inclined
to having a "spree" took advantage of the opportunity to "step out" before starting on a slow journey that would deprive him of an opportunity for
many months.

Freighting was conducted by heavily financed
companies. Huge covered wagons were outfitted
and each loaded with about three tons of freight
consigned to distant points in the west. Common
freight was flour, bacon, coffee, sugar, salt, condensed foods, clothing, shoes, guns and ammunition.
Not all freighters were permitted to carry liquor.
Each one of those big wagons was drawn by six or
eight yoke of oxen, the wheel and lead yokes were
cattle that had been broken to the yoke, but many
of the others first felt the pressure of the ox bow
at Nebraska City and were entirely wild and unbroken. Each train consisted of ten or fifteen
wagons and the working force was a wagon boss, a
cook, two night herders and a driver for each
wagon. The oxen were always called "bulls" and the
drivers "bull whackers."

The night before the train started was mostly
spent by the bull whackers in dissipation and the
day of the start found them yoking the unbroken
steers and getting them a few miles away the first
day. It may be surmised that this was no light
task and the roads were over the virgin prairie toward the northwest to a point on the Platte river

near Grand Island, thence westward. It was a rough road made worse by the passage of thousands of heavily loaded wagons. The small streams, the mud holes, the hills, fording the rivers and small streams where crossed, all tended to make the life of the "bull whacker" a worrisome affair and that of the train boss more so.

Mr. Hall was about 18 years old when he struck out to make his way in the world. He said he had helped his mother cook at home and on the strength of that applied for the position of cook for a train outfitting to leave for the west. The train boss was a competent man in most things required of the boss, but his failing was to go on a spree whenever he was in Nebraska City. He was just finishing a glorious "toot" and was lit up so that he did not get over it for a day or two, and they started with the boss almost at the point of delirium tremens. His whiskey was exhausted and none allowed on the train. By giving him great quantities of strong coffee, the boss eventually came into his own.

The boss' job was strenuous. Among other things he had to ride ahead and choose camping and feeding places and crossings over the streams. Before his nervous system had fully recovered from his recent big drunk it was desired to find a crossing over the Platte river. He chose a crossing place, and as he neared the other bank in his exploration, a party of Indians on the war path attempted to intercept him. He was so scared and unstrung that he ran back through the shallow water falling down and continuing till exhausted thinking the Indians were pursuing him while his rough neck army was rolling in the grass on the bank convulsed with laughter enjoying his frantic efforts to escape from Indians who had not pursued him.

Riding horses were supplied for the herders and for the train boss. The train boss was more exposed to danger from lurking Indians than the others because he was obliged to leave the train to find camping and feeding places and where water for the stock was available. It required good judgment to select camping places that provided all their wants and yet guard against hostile Indians.

The customs of the march were two drives a day. The night herders drove in the cattle that had been under their guard on grass during the night at about 3 A. M. and then tumbled into bed in the wagons. The drivers yoked up the cattle and the train made another drive till nine or ten o'clock A. M., when they stopped for breakfast and a rest till 3 P. M. A corral was made by the first team turning to the right to form a half circle and the second team to the left till they met, thus by all following the leader a complete circle was formed and the wheels chained together. This made a strong corral into which the live stock was driven in case of an Indian attack as well as a place to yoke the cattle in.

Mr. Hall said that as cook, his services as a hotel chef would not have been sought. Strong coffee was always served. Bacon was the reliable meat, and crackers, sour dough fried in a skillet, was what he served his guests regularly. For sugar, molasses was used to flood the sour dough and it did no good to complain about the fare because there was nothing else for them to eat unless they happened to get a buffalo.

The herders kept the stock out on grass during both night and day stops and had no other duties to perform. That would occupy their time from 10 A. M. to 3 P. M., and 10 P. M. till 3 A. M. every day. In the case of an Indian scare the stock would be rushed quickly into the corral formed by the wagon circle. The distance traveled in the two daily drives was about 15 or 20 miles.

An accomplishment the train boss must possess was to shoe the cattle if the men could not do it. The boss Mr. Hall started with, was an exceptionally good train boss for most things, but he could not shoe oxen. This Mr. Hall found he could do and was a factor in securing him the position of train boss on the next trip, regardless of his age. As an ox has a cloven hoof it requires two half shoes to each foot. An ox requiring shoes, was ranged up near the portable forge and his shoes fastened on with the hoof firmly pressed against a wagon wheel. It took some urging to place a reluctant wild steer in position and hold him there till his shoes were nailed on.

After the first round trip, Mr. Hall always had the position of train boss. At times Indians were very troublesome and after seeing no sign of them for two or three days they seemed to rise right out of the earth and were ready to try some kind of devilment. It was a constant thing for Indian boys to follow wagon trains harassing and making them all trouble possible. Sometimes, during the years Mr. Hall engaged in freighting, Indians would be-

come dangerous enough for the U. S. Government
to send escorts of soldiers to protect them. On such
occasions several trains would join together and
elect one of the train bosses, captain. Mr. Hall
served as captain several times.

In crossing the danger zone through Nebraska,
Mr. Hall had many thrilling adventures. On one
occasion the freighting company sent a relative and
his family consisting of husband, wife and several
children under their protection to make a new home
somewhere in the west. The family was an educated one and accustomed to town living but not
familiar with bull whackers ways or Indian warfare. After leaving the base of supplies, Mr. Hall
said the train was under the absolute control of the
train boss who could use any means to enforce his
authority. Of course, this family was subject to
his authority. One beautiful morning the oxen
were yoked up and started as usual at three A. M.,
the family in their spring covered wagon drawn by
mules, were with them, of course. No Indians had
been seen for days. They made their morning stop
and the family to secure a little more privacy, went
on about a third of a mile crossing a small creek
and began preparing for breakfast. The main train
had just got their cattle out on grass, when shooting and a commotion was heard where the family
had stopped, and the herders rushed the cattle back
into the wagon corral and the men went to the rescue of the man and his family. As rapidly as this
was done and in spite of the firing on the Indians
with their long range rifles, before they got there
the whole family had been murdered and scalped
and their wagon and property set fire, clothing

scattered about the prairie, the stock run off, and the Indians were out of reach. Mr. Hall said that it was a horrible and unforgettable sight to see that family killed and mutilated in such a short space of time. There they laid in their bloody garments, father, mother, and children, just where overtaken, by their fire with cooking utensils and food stuffs by them, and their bedding and property scattered, and wagon still burning.

As train boss, Mr. Hall was obliged to detach himself from the others to find watering places, pasturage and camping grounds. It was a dangerous task and he was always mounted on a good horse and heavily armed. He was many times chased back to the train by Indians who were constantly trying to ambush stragglers, or run off live stock. This Indian danger zone was largely in Nebraska, west of Grand Island.

Mr. Hall told of one of those scouting trips to find a watering place for the cattle when a war party of Indians succeeded in ambushing and surrounding him and it was with great difficulty that he escaped with his life. As a rule, the trains paid little attention to the annoyances of Indian boys but when the seasoned warriors were on the war path and went in large parties, extreme caution was necessary. On this occasion Indian war parties being active, several ox trains had united and elected Mr. Hall train captain. A platoon of U. S. soldiers under command of a Lieutenant had been detailed to guard them through the hostile zone.

One hot day the long line of wagons drawn by their several yoke of oxen was strung out a long distance toiling slowly parallel with the river two or three miles distant. The cattle began to show signs of need of water and he left the train to locate a watering place. No Indians had been seen for some time but it was known they were in a dangerous mood and raiding any unprotected traveling outfit or ranch they could safely attack. Mr. Hall was mounted on a fast running horse, but one that feared Indians and would not stand for shooting from the ground near him. He was equipped with a Henry 16-shot carbine repeater good for short distances, two holster six shooter revolvers and a six colt in his belt. He rode down to the water and had chosen a place where the cattle could be watered and was letting his horse drink. Fortunately he had not dismounted. The horse had hardly touched the water with his mouth when he raised his head in alarm and Mr. Hall saw he was entirely surrounded by a large war party of Indians who seemed certain they had him trapped.

It was impossible to ride around them and a fight was hopeless, so he decided quickly on the only way to escape. As he was riding a race horse, he hoped by rushing the middle of the circle to get through and be able to outrun the Indians. He made a dash through their line with them all shooting at him with guns and arrows but they missed him because of his speed. He was hopeful of beating them to the train but one Indian was mounted on a faster pony than his horse was and that Indian kept up the chase, as Mr. Hall said, with a pony so fast that it cut circles around his horse. The rest of the Indians were hopelessly left behind.

Then the fight was for the two and the Indian kept on the side of the pony away from Mr. Hall and would shoot arrows at him under the pony's neck. Hall emptied his Henry repeater carbine and said he could swear he could see the pony's hair through the sights. Then both holster revolvers were emptied and still the Indian was shooting arrows at him. To add to the danger they were now within gunshot of the train and the soldiers began shooting and endangered him as much as they did the Indian. Mr. Hall said he finally came to his senses and realized what he had not during the excitement. They were going so fast that the Indian was running away from his shots and he was shooting behind him all the time. Then using great care with his belt revolver he watched for the Indian's head to appear under the pony's neck to throw another arrow at him, and holding far ahead the pursuit ceased with that shot and the pony ran back to the Indians.

Mr. Hall reached the train with his temper much ruffled at the soldiers who had not ventured from the train to drive off his pursuer but had engaged in much gun-fire with their long range army guns that endangered Mr. Hall as well as the Indian without affording help. He had escaped with one severe wound, an arrow was sticking in his hip, and while it was being pulled out, a proceeding not very enjoyable, the pain did not mitigate the lecture he gave the soldiers.

The terminal of some of the long freighting trips sometimes took him to Salt Lake City and he met Brigham Young and other Mormon leaders. At one time he had a revolt among his bull whackers and they proposed to leave him in a body. They were largely a company of New York City musicians and toughs, who, desiring to go to the Pacific coast, took service as bull whackers in a cattle train. He said they were a tough bunch but made the mountains ring with music. At a point in the mountains he found that the New Yorkers were planning to desert in a body and leave him so short handed that he would be helpless to move the train. For all practical purposes the law of the plains gave the train boss absolute control over the company, even to taking life. He quelled the mutiny and stopped the rebellion at the point of a gun and had no more trouble with the New York musicians who were singing, "I am bound for California with my banjo on my knee."

The wagon freighting ceased with the completion of the U. P. railroad through to the coast, but the amount of freight that had been moved by those slow ox teams was incalculable. Among the freighters were many lawless, desperate men, but like all great undertakings there was room for clean able men to float to the top and hold positions of responsibility and trust. Mr. Hall finally responded to the natural desire of a man for a home and a settled place of abode. He married the daughter of one of the most prosperous grain and stock farmers near Nebraska City, and set up a ranch of his own in Boone county. He became widely known and universally respected, and did his part in developing the state during its formative stage. The distance to a school house was a drawback to his location, but he surmounted that by hiring a teacher to instruct his growing family at their own home.

I know of no one who may be credited with the kind of development that eastern and central Nebraska owes to the great freighting movement than it owes to Edward Hall. I believe every word he told of his experiences was true. His modesty permitted him to leave this world of activities without recording his great experience as plainsman and freighter and I feel that in recording what he told me I become an interested bystander, only one degree removed.

CHAPTER XVI

A Pioneer Preacher

"A man he was to all the country dear,
And passing rich with forty pounds a year."
—*Goldsmith.*

REV. Charles Wesley Wells, a Methodist minister, gave many interesting experiences he had among the early Nebraska settlers in a book entitled "A Frontier Life." He met the same hardships and trials that homesteaders did while he served the charges to which he was sent. In his capacity of pastor, like the pioneer doctor, he had abundant opportunity to see the different phases of pioneer Nebraska life because their homes were always open to his visits and it was his duty to visit them.

Rev. Wells was undeniably a Nebraska pioneer. His early life found him fighting Indians or hunting buffalo in the South Platte country, and after obeying the call to preach, he spent his first years between Beatrice and Red Cloud when settlers were so distant from each other that he sometimes would not pass a home in an all day travel. More than once while a young man, did he go to sleep supperless on the open prairie with the stars for a roof and his horse picketed nearby where it could find grass to eat.

He was sent to the Lyons charge in northeastern Nebraska and among other feats hauled driftwood from the Missouri river, 15 miles distant to provide his household fuel and gave half of it to a member of his church for providing the horses to haul it. He usually reported from $132.000 to $400.00 received on salary for the year.

Later while on the Albion charge in Boone county, he said that most of the congregation lived in sod houses or dugouts and described some of them. He said one of the prosperous farmers on the Cedar river valley had a house 36 feet long and 12 feet wide in which two families, two cook stoves, two tables and five beds found space. The walls were six feet high, the roof composed of poles, brush, coarse hay and sods, and the floor was simply dirt. Here the two families lived, cooked, ate and slept and many times the preacher and family stayed with them, making three families. Such crowding-up was common among settlers themselves when night found them away from home.

At another place where he and his wife and little girl stayed, the sod house was made as neat and tidy as the housewife could make it by hard work. In the night the bedbugs came out of the coarse hay, brush and dirt of the house roof and attacked them so that they could scarcely sleep. Be the house-keeper ever so careful she could not banish the bed-bugs from a house where there was a roof and ceiling of this kind.

Rev. Wells brings his readers into the innermost sanctity of the early settlers' homes. Their hardships, as well as the fortitude it took to serve a congregation during the homestead days are made plain in his recital of his reception on the Norfolk charge, and the hardships to secure fuel and shelter incident to both preacher and laymen. In his book he said that he expected to be returned to the

Lyons charge because the brethren requested it, the presiding elder promised it, and he had a sick baby that was not well enough to endure the hardships of moving. Never-the-less an eastern preacher who had come to the conference on trial and would not go farther west, was given the more advanced Lyon charge and Rev. Wells was sent to the new one at Norfolk. After driving three days through bad weather and muddy roads he reached Norfolk. His reception and experiences are well told in his own words as follows:

"As there were no railroads running through this country to Norfolk, our new field of labor, we hired a brother to take our goods through with a team, and I took my wife and children in the buggy. Before starting to our new field, our presiding elder instructed us to go to a Brother G., about two miles from the town where we were to make our home. Here he said we would find a Methodist home, where we could stay until ready to go to housekeeping. With Mrs. Wells in poor health and a sick babe, we traveled three days through the mud and cold, hoping to find a welcome when at our journey's end. On reaching Norfolk late in the afternoon, we met a local preacher, who kindly directed us to Brother G.'s house, which the presiding elder had recommended to us as a home until our goods should arrive. Late in the evening, cold and hungry, and with a sick child, we called at Brother G.'s, made ourselves known, and were very coolly invited into the house. On first arriving, we found that Brother G. was not at home, and thought, perhaps, when he arrived, our reception would be different. He soon came home from his work, but, instead of bringing sunshine with him, the clouds were thicker and blacker than ever. He gave us no encouragement whatever, but by his actions made us understand that we were not welcome, even to the circuit, much less to his home. The meal being ready, we were invited to the dining room, where we ate our supper alone. After we were through, and had left the room the family sat down and ate. We consoled ourselves somewhat by the thought that in the morning it would be different; but in the morning we sat down to breakfast alone, and the family ate theirs, as before. This was not done because of the want of room or need of dishes, for they had an abundance of both; but it was done to make it appear that we were a great burden on their hands. The lady of the house claimed to be unwell, and not able to do the work. Mrs. Wells offered to help about the housework, but the good sister, by her actions, gave her to understand that she didn't want any of her help. Though Brother G. was looked upon as one of the leading Methodists of that country, he gave no word of encouragement regarding the work, and said, "There is no house where you can live; neither is there any chance for a support on the charge." Though young in the ministry, I had gone through too many rough places to be backed down in this way. But for my wife and children, I should have gone to a barn or hay stack and slept, rather than stay over night where I was not welcome.

"Soon after breakfast we drove to town to search for a house to live in, and to look after our goods, which we expected that day. Hearing of a young lawyer by the name of Robertson, who was a Methodist, we hunted him up, introduced ourselves, and told him what we wanted. He seemed to be very glad to see us, gave us a very warm reception and said, "Yes, we will find you a house." In less than half an hour he came to us with the information that he had found a house into which we could move at any time. Not knowing how coolly we were treated at G.'s he advised us to go back there and stay until our goods should arrive. As apparently we were not wanted, to return and stay another night was a hard pill to take; but as we had no money to spend at the hotel, and our babe was sick, we felt it was the only thing to be done at the time. Besides, we had left some of our things at Brother G.'s, which required us to go there anyhow. On our way back, we met Mrs. G., wading through the mud toward a neighbor's, and she informed us that we would find our things on the porch. On telling her that our goods had not come, and we did not know where to go, she said, "I am not able to wait on you any longer." She was footing it away from home to get rid of us, working much harder than she need have done for us at home. Going to the house, we found our goods on the porch, and the doors locked as against a thief. Previous to this we had thought it possible that this unkindness was only imaginary on our part, but now there was no mistake. They didn't want us, and had turned us out of doors.

"The reader may know something of our feelings when he reflects that we were among strangers, with but little money, a very sick child, and no shelter from the night air. Surely this was one of the greatest trials of my life. If an enemy had thus turned us from his house, we could have endured it much better; but it was one who should have been our best friend. If I mistake not, this brother was a steward in the Methodist church at that time.

"Notwithstanding this great annoyance, we laughed over our predicament, and returned to the town where we met a good local brother, who lived five or six miles in the country. After telling him how the presiding elder had directed us to Brother G.'s, and how we had been treated by Brother G., he sent us to his home, and there we were received right royally. This brother's name is John Allberry, a local preacher, whom we shall ever hold in grateful remembrance for his kindness. Brother Allberry was a poor man, but had a large heart. Though he lived in a small house, he made us feel at home and far more comfortable than if he had possessed all the needed room and conveniences, without a good, warm welcome. After getting my family under shelter, appointments were made for Sunday preaching. The morning appointment was at the Cunningham schoolhouse, where I found friends by the score. Brother Cunningham was a well-to-do farmer, though not a church member at the time. He took great interest in our welfare, perhaps for the sake of his wife, who was one of the leading Methodists of that community, and who always delighted to make the preacher and his family feel at home in her house.

"After a few days' waiting, our goods came, and we were keeping house on our new field of labor. Our ill-treatment made for us many friends, and perhaps gave us access to the hearts of the people as nothing else could have done. We moved into the rooms of an old hotel building, which was rusty, dirty and cold. We could endure this, when supplied with fuel for the fire and something to eat. In knocking around from place to place in the cold, damp weather, our sick babe continued to grow worse, and in one short week after settling in Norfolk he died. Again we were smitten with sorrow. Here we were, far from home, among entire strangers, and our little child torn from our bosoms. But this new and deep affliction called around us many friends, who ministered to us in our sorrow, and buried our little one on the hillside in the Norfolk cemetery, where its little form still lies and where our parental hearts often go to weep. After making the acquaintance of the people on the entire charge, we were well pleased with our circuit. I was the first traveling preacher sent to that charge by the Conference, though Brother Beels, a local preacher, had served in the previous year.

"The fall season passed off pleasantly and quietly, and we enjoyed our work. The trials we passed through at the outset better prepared us for others that might follow. We had four regular appointments, with preaching at each every two weeks. Winter set in early, and was long and severe, which caused us considerable suffering. I say suffering; for we did suffer from the cold. We did a great deal of traveling in the bitter weather; but this we didn't mind so much as having to suffer from the cold when at home. Our house was an unfinished frame building, and exceedingly airy. Besides a house exposed to the winds, we had the poorest of fuel. There being no coal in the country, we burned such wood as the brethren could bring to us, principally green cottonwood. Whoever has tried burning green cottonwood for winter fuel will know how we fared during the severe weather. The only way we could keep fire at all in the coldest weather was having a good supply in the house, and, while a part was burning, the rest would be thawing and drying. In this way, by continually crowding the stove with wood, we managed to avoid freezing. Sometimes during the severest weather our wood pile gave out, and I would have to replenish it with my own hands. About a half mile up the river there was a large plum thicket, with many dead bushes. When we were out of wood, I took a long rope and my ax, went to this place, cut down dead plum bushes, piled them on the ice in the river, tied the rope about them, and dragged them on the ice to the house, which was only a few rods from the river. In this way I could draw an immense pile of brush, especially when the ice was smooth.

"The crops having been destroyed by drouth and grasshoppers during the summer, it seemed almost impossible that many of the people could get through the winter. Taking into consideration the condition of the preachers and churches on the frontier work, our presiding elder went East, and solicited money, goods and provisions for the people, and especially for the preachers' families. Had he not done so, we should have seen much harder times, or been compelled to abandon our work. Goods were shipped to me to use whatever was needed for my family, and the rest was to be given to the most needy around us. In this way many were helped through the winter. The preachers throughout our Western country were helped in this way, and it was made possible for them to remain at their work.

"We received financial aid in another way while on this charge. I drove a four-horse team nearly through one harvesting of small grain. The Lord, in thus giving me something to do at which I could earn a few dollars, helped me to provide for my family. Some may think it disgraceful for a minister to work in the harvest field, but I enjoyed it, and felt it quite an honor to be able to do so much for myself. Want did not compel me to go to work in the harvest field, but we had a scanty supply, and I thought this would help fill our larder and do no harm further than taking me from my studies. I have always told the brethren that I had good, strong, and willing hands, and, if need be, could make my living by manual labor. The good Lord, however, has always provided a way, and I have never been compelled to leave the ministry in order to make a living, though, at times my family has had scanty rations and but little of the luxuries of life. Many times, during this Conference year, we have sat down to the table with only bread and coffee for breakfast; at other times our meal consisted of bread and butter alone, without tea, coffee or sugar. At the beginning of my ministry I adopted the rule of not going into debt for anything when it could be avoided. Because of this rule, we were sometimes for weeks without sugar in the house, excepting a little Mrs. Wells laid by in case of sickness or other emergencies.

"During the winter of this Conference year we had some good revival meetings, and many were taken into the church. I suppose I am best adapted to border work, and, if so, there is where I ought to be.

"Sometime during the year another appointment was made at a little town called Pierce, in Pierce county. Mine was the first Methodist preaching, and probably the first preaching of any kind in this little town.

"At the opening of spring we moved into a house on a farm, a short distance from town, where we had better accommodation than in the old tenement house.

"After the presiding elder had removed the brother from the Madison charge, and placed it in my care, we removed to Madison, because there was a parsonage at that place, which, though small, was better than living in a rented house. This was our fourth move in less than two years. In moving into all kinds of houses we find all kinds of insects that prey upon human blood. One house we found as nearly alive with bugs as a house could be, and not walk off. Soon after going to bed the first night, the bugs sallied out upon us by the hundreds, as if we were sent there on purpose to feed them. Wife and I heroically defended ourselves and child from the invaders by killing them as fast as they charged upon us, not allowing too many to get hold of us at once; for they acted as if they intended to carry us to their hiding place for future use. After killing the first squad that came out of ambush, we began to count as fast as we destroyed them, and by actual count we killed more than two hundred besides the many we had deprived of life before beginning to count. Some people have a great dread of certain kinds of bugs, especially such as creep into houses and get into bed with them; but if they were as well acquainted with these innocent little creatures as are the frontier preachers of the Western country, they would know that their bite is not always fatal, though sometimes they do cause considerable suffering.

"This year I reported one hundred and three members for the Norfolk and Madison circuits, and received one hundred and thirty dollars on salary. The grasshoppers had taken a greater portion of my salary claim and eaten it up, so we had to be satisfied with what they left. Spiritually and socially this had been a very pleasant year, but, financially, among the hardest in all my ministry; for now I had a family to support, and needed more than when alone."

Rev. Wells had been assigned to Albion in 1877. The first homestead filed on in the county had been taken in 1871. There was not a single church building of any denomination in the county and services were held in sod houses. When he first reached Albion he helped build a parsonage that was the first church building erected by any denomination in the county. It was dedicated by a donation party and the marriage of a prominent farmer blacksmith to a girl who had accompanied the preacher from Madison county. The frame house having been lightly made, very nearly collapsed under the weight of the guests who had assembled in the unfinished chamber to witness the marriage ceremony.

CHAPTER XVII

The Weekly Newspaper
Pioneer Poets

"A chiel's amang you takin' notes,
And, faith, he'll prent it."
—*Burns*

IN close comradeship with the sod house, the breaking plow, the public school where pupils under the eighth grade were instructed, was the pioneer weekly newspaper. Like the pioneer water mill that ground the settlers' wheat into coarse flour between the stone "burrs" of the old time flouring mill, the weekly newspaper was a part of the homemakers economy to help ferment and mould the policies of people into being, as the primitive farm tools moulded and placed the fertile land in a condition to bring prosperity and opulence to the settlers' children, if he passed away before his hopes for material benefits had been fulfilled.

Some of those printing establishments of sod house days were exceedingly meager in the matter of equipment. I once saw a printing establishment that had arrived at a spot that public rumor had decided would be a town location. Two young men rode in, in a shaky one-seated, one-horse, no-top buggy. The paint had vanished from the wood work of the vehicle under exposure to the sun and the tires on the wheels were so loose that they rattled cheerily as the old white, swayback horse painfully rambled along. Yet that buggy carried the personal belongings of the embryo Horace Greeleys who had "gone west" to better their condition. The entire "makins" of the start of a future city daily paper was packed under the seat of that old buggy.

Once two high school boys who had served apprenticeship as "devil" in my country printing shop, pooled their earnings that amounted to the fabulous sum of $20 and bought equipment and started a daily paper that existed for several months. They uncovered a broken down army press somewhere and bought a small amount of bruised and discarded type including a raid on the "hell" box in both town printing offices, and the daily paper was born. To explain what an army press was known to be at the time would be to recall that during the Civil war, headquarters at army concentration points used a small press to print headquarters orders on. The press worked something like the first mimeographs that were operated by hand. Possibly the makers of the first mimeograph took inspiration from the army press. By taking time, because the process was slow, the boys manipulated it and they were rich with unoccupied time.

It may be well to explain what "hell" type was. In the current vocabulary of the printing office at the time when all newspaper matter was set by hand, and linotypes were not yet known, any type that accidently fell on the floor or became bruised was seldom returned to the case, but found its way into a box provided for holding damaged metal slugs and type. When enough damaged metal accumulated to warrant the expense of shipping it to a type foundry it was exchanged for new type. A great deal of type was required to set the more pretentious papers before machine setting was invented, and great amounts of "pi" and damaged type found a haven in the "hell" box. Be it known that the "nomen" hell was heard oftener than heaven in those early day printing shops. Perhaps the consciences of the printers wandered that way the most. Many of them were a sad lot.

The county I lived in was very young when a bright young lawyer wandered into the county seat village and gathered up the scattered type a predecessor had left in storage and started a weekly paper. He brought with him only a smattering knowledge of law but an exalted knowledge of the taste of whiskey which he diligently cultivated till he attained perfection in that line. But his libations finally called him in and the paper had to be sold. On an impulse I made a bid and as my bid of $475 cash for the entire equipment, subscription list and good will was the highest bid, especially as an all cash bid was not easily assembled in those days, I became a publisher and editor at once. That was April 1, 1885.

The only good piece of furniture or equipment, barring the Washington hand press, was an office desk that the editor's wife had paid $25 for to present to her husband on his birthday anniversary. The Washington press was a replica of the one Benjamin Franklin invented, and to do those presses justice it may be said that they never wore out and would do good work under all conditions if handled by an expert. The impression could be made strong enough to almost squeeze the sap out of an elm plank, or it might be delicate enough to print a dainty calling card. Many a day I sat near the press on press day and folded and addressed by hand, the entire weekly edition of 600 or 700 papers while my two printers were doing the printing. The forms would be lying on the press bed and one man at the side held a long roller well inked that he would run across the forms and back. The pressman standing on the other side would feed in a sheet of paper under the grippers then turn a crank and roll the forms under the platen and then reach for the big lever and pull it down on the forms. The heavy weight that came down with a sort of corkscrew movement did the press work thoroughly. The lever was then released and permitted to return to its original position. The press was rolled back by a reverse movement of the crank, the printed paper removed, and was ready for folding and the press ready for the next sheet.

The office was equipped as most country plants were. There was "burgeois" type enough to set a few columns of reading matter and "nonpareil" to set legals, and a small amount of display type, some having faces mashed by too close acquaintance with the Washington press or the wabbly old job press. Some fonts were lacking in sorts and when a certain letter was exhausted it was common to put in another misfit font type. Sometimes a loyal supporter of the paper let his ad run for months without change, using the same type. The type used was what printers called "bastard" size and foundries did not make type of uniform size. Later those irregular sizes were abolished and the point system provided uniformity. Only a limited supply of leads were kept for thin spacing of type but all slugs and heavy spacing was done by using strips of wood made from cigar boxes. As civilization brought in schools, it also brought cigars with the first comers, so the country newspaper never lacked material for slugs and leads.

In this office was a small job press that had been through much experience. There was no throw off lever and power was provided by a foot treadle. If something accidently fell on the forms or the operator was not quick enough in feeding the sheets of paper under the grippers there was no stopping the machine. Something foreign of a substantial nature had fallen on the forms once during a period of irresponsibility on the part of the printer. The accident followed after he had been standing before the bar of public opinion in a saloon, taking a double portion of his customary invigorator. As he was not quick enough to retrieve the piece of metal and it got the full force of the press, it mashed a row of type, sprung the press bed and dislocated one of the press arms. Hence forward it mashed type with great abandon and the work turned off, to say the least, was not artistic.

The paper cutter consisted of a shoe knife and straight edge measuring stick. Paper requiring to be cut to fit a job was placed on a board table, the straight edge adjusted to the size of sheet desired and the shoe knife drawn across on the line till the sheets of paper were reduced to proper size. The quoins to lock up the forms were small blocks of wood, and a shooting stick, an iron about nine inches long with a notched end was propelled by a wooden mallet to lock up the forms. The usual sized paper was an eight column folio, half already printed when the paper was bought. They were affectionately called "patent insides." The night before press day, those sheets were laid out on a flat table or board platform, and every few layers well wet down and by next day all would be moist and ready for the press. The Washington hand press printed better when the paper was damp while modern power presses must print the paper dry to get best results.

After the paper was all printed the cleaning up process consisted of first placing the heavy forms in a wooden box made with a slanting back and drain, much resembling a kitchen sink, only it provided for the forms to stand nearly upright. The type was then thoroughly brush scrubbed with cold water made very strong with Lewis lye to cleanse the type of ink and specks of paper. They were allowed to drain over night. In winter the wooden quoins and cigar box slugs having been thoroughly wet in the washing process would be frozen and the forms as solid as a sheet of ice by morning. As the water pail, ink, and everything freezable was stiff with ice in the morning, great care had to be observed in thawing out the forms and distributing the type. As every type had a box and font of its own, it took Friday and Saturday to put the type back in the boxes they came from and clean up and replace furniture and be ready to begin setting type for the next paper on the following Monday morning.

In this office my entire force of employes consisted of a man and a small boy who "rolled" for the paper press day at a salary of fifty cents a week.

The boy added to his stipend by selling old papers for five cents a dozen. On assuming ownership, I found that he was industriously selling the files of the paper when the demand for old papers exceeded the supply. His title was "office devil," and like many other great men who started with a humble beginning, the last I heard of him he was superintendent of a big division of the International Harvester Co. But the man who was the steady help was practically the whole office force.

James Hall was a man well along in the forties, of generous physique, and weighed about 240 pounds. He was a typical printer of his day with all the print shop superstitions and habits, a tramp printer by trade and a hard drinker by practice. His capacity for carrying whiskey in his anatomy was never challenged by others, not excepting members of the printing fraternity whose prowess in that line was always recognized. Hall was a philosopher and ready with an answer and excuse. At the time he was in my employ, the printing office towel was the subject of much and wide spread comment as an instrument of fearsome power as a weapon of offense or defense because it became so hard by usage and was never washed. Neither was the printing office floor ever scrubbed. In defense of my attempt to have Hall scrub the composing room floor he gazed at me pityingly over his glasses and informed me that he never, in all his long experience, knew but once of a printing office floor being scrubbed. That occasion was the Lincoln Journal when pick axes and spades were utilized and many pounds of "hell" type was recovered.

Hall's aversion to setting too much type was not denied. His contention was that one galley was as much as the public expected and that they much preferred to read the display ads, that had been greatly amplified with cigar box slugs. I soon discovered that Hall, regardless of his Herculean build, was an arrant coward, even though he had surrounded a pint of whiskey. At the time I was under-nourished and only weighed 125 pounds. I told Hall that I should supply him with editorials to set that might provoke violence, and I was not built for fighting, and he was. I expected that he would be ready to fight should the office be invaded. He gazed disapprovingly over his glasses at me and said earnestly, "Mr. Barns, I always thought it was more honorable to run than to fight." A few days later I came into the shop somewhat out of humor and saw him writing something that a big Irishman who had been posted for getting drunk, seemed to be dictating. I dispersed the meeting and later found that Hall had been writing a retraction of what had offended the Irishman, for me to publish. He afterward fixed it up with the irrate Irishman by advising him not to provoke me to wrath, but keep his distance. That I was a dirty fighter, not depending on ordinary means of defense, not even a gun, but would use a knife without mercy.

One cold winter Friday morning Hall's libations the night before made him sleep late and he found the forms he had left to drain after washing them with cold water and lye, were frozen tight together. Therefore, he stood them against the stove to thaw out but the slant was too great or fire too warm, or the cigar box slugs shrunk abnormally when the

thawing took place, anyway the whole forms fell out,
all sizes of type and slugs in a mass of "pi" well
known as the climax of disaster to any old time
printer. For a printer of his day, Hall had committed an almost criminal offense and he gathered
his grip containing his change of socks and started
to leave town, walking on the railroad track. He
was thinly clad and the weather frightfully cold, so
that he soon realized that he was cutting his base
of supplies and so returned to the wreck.

At the time every country paper was a political
organ. Hall was a republican and I had made the
paper a reliably democratic sheet with homestead
land office notices under the Cleveland administration looming up like a peach at the end of a row a
lazy boy was hoeing. I heard Hall in a discussion ad-
vocating Cleveland democracy, with fervency. I
asked for the explanation and why the commendable
change. His response was that he believed when a
newspaper changed hands or changed policy, the
printers were transferred with the newspaper. The
time came when Hall followed the custom of the
printers of his day and went on the road again as
a tramp printer. Somewhere over in Michigan he
had apparently just recovered from an alcoholic de-
bauch and wrote a letter to me in Nebraska an-
nouncing his permanent withdrawal from the republican party. I thought best to give his conver-
sion wide publicity as an example of a victim saved
from the burning. This was disputed by his former
fellow party men who claimed that he had aposta-
tized long before.

But the press of Nebraska, augmented by able
city dailies that soon began to function, were a

strong help in developing the state and advertising to the world the possibilities of success for young, strong people, who would throw in with the settlers and bring their activities and energies with them.

* * *

The stirring scenes in Nebraska during homestead days did little to encourage romance, poetry or music. The windy, dusty days, blizzards, grasshoppers, Indians, bull whackers, gun fighters, gamblers, and saloon attractions among those in town and the poor homesteaders living in a hole in the side of a hill and drinking water from a "cistern" that was no more than a hole washed out of the bottom of a ravine during a heavy rainfall, was not a fertile ground on which to grow poets. The politics of the railroads with their pass bribery and other doubtful enterprises natural to red blooded, vigorous young men who knew little restraint, did not tend to develop romance and sentiment.

Out of all this debatable environment came John M. Thurston. He possessed natural ability, but his education was limited. He was a natural orator and a product of the West. He had gained a smattering knowledge of law and had much practical experience among the politicians. His ability to move audiences and shrewdness as a manipulator of knotty questions in political caucus and convention gave him a position with the Union Pacific railroad management. He was made chief counsel for the road at what was at the time a fabulous salary of $10,000 a year, with able lawyers to assist him in determining legal matters that arose from time to time. The politics of the state was built on the republican party foundation but the real contentions were between the interests of the Union Pacific and Burlington & Missouri railroads in Nebraska. Added to Thurston's ability to sway audiences by his eloquence, was his ability to mix personally with the politicians and successfully lobby the legislatures in the interests of his employers. That also extended to the members of the so-called third house of the legislature and the lobbyists and politicians among whom a man who did not drink whiskey was an unknown quantity, and an outcast.

Many stories are told about Thurston's hunting prairie chickens, trick shooting with a rifle and the ease with which he could hit a nickle tossed in the air with his rifle addition to his shotgun. He was also a favorite in popular drinking and carousing with the practical jokers throughout the state. Eventually Thurston became United States senator and an influential member of the National republican party. Thurston once presided at a republican national convention. He must have possessed a poetic mind that he hesitated to develop among the practical jokers and rough neck politicians with whom he was constantly associated. He gave out one poem that showed that he possessed real poetic talent but it was received with such a shower of rough jokes and sarcastic criticisms that he never made a second attempt. Here is his one effort:

To the Rose

I said to the rose, Oh Rose, Sweet Rose;
    Will you lie on my breast tonight,
Will you nestle there, with your perfume rare,
    And your petals pure and white?

I said to the rose, Oh Rose, Sweet Rose;
      Will you thrill to my every sigh,
Tho' your life exhale in the morning pale,
      And you wither and fade and die?

I said to the rose, Oh Rose, Sweet Rose;
      Will you throb with my every breath;
Will you give me the bliss of a passionate kiss,
      Albeit, the end is death?

The white rose lifted her stately head
      And answered me fair and true;
I am happy and blest to lie on your breast
      For the woman who gave me to you.

There were so many parodies on this sentimental
poem and Thurston suffered so much from the practical jokes of his pioneer associates that he never
again gave out a poem of any kind. At the
time the rose poem was given to the world, there
were two Nebraska newspaper men who had taken
out their papers as pioneer poets. Their talents
consisted partly in taking the skeleton of a poem
some one had composed and clothe it in their own
unique style. It was like the skeleton of a farmer's
scarecrow, and they dressed it with many colored
coats, even though they left it like the imitation
man, all ragged and forlorn, but really a praise-
worthy scarecrow. Their parodies certainly helped
kill Senator Thurston's poetic aspirations. One of
these parody fiends was Doc Bixby of the Lincoln
Journal, and the other Will Maupin, widely known
as a writer. Here is what Doc Bixby gave birth to:

I said to my nose, Oh Nose, Red Nose;
    Will you say to me, honor bright,
What the hidden cause in the matter was
    That you came to such a sight?

I said to my nose, Oh Nose, Red Nose;
    You shame me at every turn,
And whene'er I am in the hot old sun,
    You blister and blaze and burn.

I said to my nose, Oh Nose, Red Nose;
    Is there any relief in reach?
Is there any old dye that I can buy
    That will work as a nasal bleach?

The red nose lifted its self a notch,
    And answered me, "Aber nit:"
If you drink less grog and more water, hog,
    It would whiten me up a bit.

Then Will Maupin struck his hatchet into the war post and the following parody on the Rose appeared on the prairies of Nebraska:

I said to my lunch, Oh Lunch, Late Lunch;
    Will you lie on my stomach tonight;
Will you nestle there or rear and tear,
    In a huge nightmarish fright?

I said to my lunch, Oh Lunch, Late Lunch;
    Will you thrill me with aching pain;
Will your fits and jerks bust my stomach works
    So I can never lunch again?

I said to my lunch, Oh Lunch, Late Lunch;
  Will you throb like a stone bruised toe;
Will you double me up like a poisoned pup,
  And fill me with grief and woe?

And my lunch gave a dyspeptic hump;
  And answered me fair and true;
I'm onto my job and I'll throb and jump,
  Till the air with your cussing's blue.

Of course Nebraska had many poets later but the tendency was for early Nebraska people to turn to practical things. As a pioneer editor I had some wonderful poetry given me for publication co-incident with the departure of some good man or woman or angelic child, that no one could make parodies on.

The sod house environments with the fleas, bedbugs, twisted hay and rosin weed fires and lack of credit at the grocery store was not conducive to the development of poets.

CHAPTER XVIII

The Money Loaner

"Here lies old four per cent;
The more he grabbed, the more he lent.
The more he lent, the more he craved.
My God, can such a man be saved?"
—*A money shark's epitaph.*

THAT the period of agricultural development required financing was as undisputed as that of a transportation system, to place the products of the soil on a distant market must function or the grain on the best farming portion of the new state must waste on the ground where it was grown. Territorial Nebraskans found timber along the Missouri river to make log houses, lumber and fuel. Bankers came with the early settlers and the Missouri river gave transportation. It was for the early period of statehood to venture farther from the river onto the treeless prairie, there to develop the grain growing section that ante-dated the fattening of domestic animals. The banker and money loaner was as necessary as the settler and played as important a part in the changing of the west from wilderness to civilization. It required money as well as industry, courage and brawn to make the change.

Among the first problems to be solved by the early territorial immigrants was banking. It was not so much a problem of the sod house period as it was the log house period along the Missouri river. Every phase of banking was tried by the early settlers who had more energy, activity and push than they

had money.   Among early records the Morton history deals fully with banking problems that include
all grades known from private, corporate, and wildcat banking, from the most disreputable, unscrup-
ulous, dangerous methods, to substantial and honest
banking.   Under   shelter   of   banking there arose
numerous private loan agencies that charged enormous interest.   To avoid prosecutions for usury,
they took the interest from the money they loaned
and called it discount.   The territorial rather than
the state pioneers, had to face and settle vicious and
dishonest banking problems ·but usurious interest
was charged by the banks for many years of early
statehood and collected in advance under the name
of discounting.   But what the legitimate bankers
did to the poor settlers was but a mote in the eye
compared with the beam placed by the private loan
agents who continued to function till after the populist uprising during the nineties.

A settler of the sod house period on his arrival
at his destination halted his prairie schooner, that
contained his family and personal property, at some
convenient camping place and sought to locate a
quarter section of government land that he might
file a homestead claim upon.   Sometimes a locater
for a small fee helped him, and sometimes an ac-
commodating settler directed him to a desirable
tract of land.   The filing fee was small but must be
sent to the nearest U. S. Land Office.   Once located,
a sod house and stable soon rose and the family
was housed.   Improvements came slowly.   The sod
was plowed for fire guards and a garden patch.   A
water supply was imperative.   First it was brought
in barrels from a running stream, a neghbor's well,

or rain water from a washed out hole in a ravine. Very soon an open well was dug and after the thick layer of clay or loess was penetrated the sand below was found to be an unfailing storage for good water. No curbing was required but a box made of boards sunk in the sand made a reservoir for the water to gather in at the bottom of the well. A rope, log windlass, and two iron-bound buckets were needed and this required an outlay of money that the settler lacked. The need of the well convinced him that it was worthy to make sacrifices for.

Equipping the well, securing a breaking plow or boards for his sod house door, or the windows, may have been his incentive to make his first acquaintance with a banker or loan broker. The nearest banker may have been located in a town either far or near, but the banker and the borrower were strangers. Respectfully and timidly the settler entered the presence of the great man with much trepidation. The banker might have his place of business in one side of a small frame building and use the other side for a home for his wife and children. The request for a small loan to finance the well or buy a few boards, or possibly a cow or pig, was met by a demand to list the property he had for security. In the end, a demand note for $25, $50, or in extreme cases $100, would be made with the settler's horses, harness and wagon for chattel security. If the loan was granted, it was signed by the borrower and his wife, who usually joined in guaranteeing the payment of the note.

If interest above 12 per cent per annum was charged it was classed as usury. Favorable bank interest for loans below $100 was 24 per cent per

annum or 2 per cent a month. Taking the large
loan of $100 for example, the note would mature in
three months, bearing 12 per cent interest per annum. As the note only bore 12 per cent per annum
interest the 24 per cent must be taken in advance.
12 per cent interest on $100 for three months would
be only $3.00 and when the borrower was given $97
for his $100 loan, he was satisfied. In his ignorance
of banking and money loaning he failed to take into
account that the note matured in three months and
that while $3.00 was not a great sum when com-
puted for three months, it attained great proportions if computed for three years. And as a rule
that note hung on with renewals for several years.

The pioneer banker was no dullard and his wits
were sharpened to meet all conditions. A renewal
request was certain in three months unless the settler secured some teaming or prairie sod breaking
to earn the money to take up the note. To realize
from crops could not be done in that time and it
was poor farming to break prairie for others to
plant to crops and neglect to break and crop his own
land. A careful examination of the note he had
signed and pledged his horses for payment, would
show that while the interest was named at 12 per
cent per annum, a penalty of 24 per cent held
against his property in case he failed to meet his
note when it became due. While 24 per cent would
constitute usury if charged as interest, a flexible but
convenient finding of the courts was that the 24 per
cent was collectable as penalty, but could not be if
called interest. The spiritual descendant of Shy-
lock had his bond. Should he declare it forfeit, as
he did many times, the team remained in town and

the settler walked home poorer than when he filed on his homestead claim.

But most bankers were not heartless. As a rule they listened to the appeals for an extension of the note and that the borrower be given an opportunity to pay the note. The development of the country must not be overlooked. Human kindness, sympathy and helpfulness, was to be found among bankers as well as heartlessness, selfishness and narrow-mindedness. Dishonest and grasping bankers were not lacking nor were dishonest, indolent and worthless settlers, scarce. As a rule the banker met the borrower in a kindly helpful spirit, if he was worthy.

A story went the rounds illustrating the appeal for a renewal, and other favorable considerations, on a note that was notoriously past due at the bank. Being on the carpet the second or third time the borrower was working for another stand off and intimated that at the previous interview the banker had encouraged him that a continuance would be granted. The surprised banker inquired in what way he had given the encouragement. The borrower affirmed that at the former interview while he was pleading his case, he felt certain that his appeal would be granted by the generous banker because he plainly saw the glint of human kindness in his eye. As the banker had a glass eye, the eye sight of the borrower may not have failed, but his conclusions were faulty. At the conclusion of the last interview the banker's eye only carried a cold, glassy, unsympathetic stare.

The common interest rates charged by a pioneer state bank was one per cent a month to a favored few well to do farmers or business men. Frequent renewals made the rate exceed the 12 per cent per annum; 18 to 24 per cent annual interest was computed as one and a half and two per cent a month. The banks were usually sound, having survived the wildcat territorial banking days.

Those who could not get credit at banks were numerous. It was to serve this class of borrowers that brought the country loan broker, who loaned money on chattels, into prominence. The country towns were infested with young lawyers who had to struggle hard to gain a livelihood. Naturally, they took on chattel loaning as a side line to help supply their own bread line. Sometimes the loan broker was a young man who loathed work and was trying to live by his wits. Neither of those classes had money of their own but were able to interest someone to furnish them the money for a division of the profits. Sometimes an elderly person had a small stake that he sought to gain a greater income from by loaning it out to the needy on chattel security, but he was apt to be cautious.

A notable example of the way young lawyers added to their income by loaning some one money was that of a lawyer in a country town during the rising of the farmers in a movement to withdraw from the two national political parties, and form a party of their own known as the Peoples Independent party, or as they were commonly called, "Populists." He joined the movement and succeeded in being elected to office, first as governor and then supreme court judge. Before the populist movement brought him into public prominence, he secured money from some one who desired to make

his money earn more than the legal interest rate
and made loans to farmers on chattels. The loan
brokers were very objectionable to the farmers,
many of whom had suffered from the usurious interest they had been compelled to pay and the ul-
timate loss of their security. The political fights
were bitter and the line was sharply drawn between
the farmers and the two old parties, largely against
the dominant republican party, that the Lincoln
State Journal represented.

A. L. Bixby was a popular writer on the Journal
staff. He knew the ills the settlers had suffered and
had tried his hand at editing weekly papers in their
interests, till the barrenness of his own cupboard
impelled him to take service on the Journal. He
was a poet and humorist. Sometimes he spoke in
rhyme and sometimes he just spoke, but it was always humorous and touched the spot and was effective because of its unique presentation. He did
not betray his former associates but his quaint
humor uncovered their weaknesses in a way that
woke up both sides. His verse, representing the
settlers cry of despair,

"I cannot sing the old songs,
My heart is full of woe;
But I can howl calamity
From Hell to Broken Bow,"

became a war cry.

When the former lawyer loan broken became a
candidate for governor, a chattel mortgage he had
made to a farmer who borrowed money at a liberal
interest rate per month, recited that a cow called
"Speck" and a black boar pig were pledged as security for payment. Whether the interest was four

per cent a month and whether the property pledged
was taken in payment was not so much in question
as the recorded proof that the candidate had engaged in the nefarious business of a loan shark. It
was spread over the length and breadth of the state
that year and for many years, and that cow
Speck and boar black pig became famous and a
household word. The offense was forgiven because
of the humor of description.

Thousands of loan brokers made thousands of
loans resembling the loan secured by the cow Speck
and boar black pig. That loan represented a class,
not an instance. It was reported of a woman who
married late in life and came to Nebraska, that her
younger days had been spent working in a New
England factory and she had saved some money
from her frugal earnings.

Like many others she was enticed by the opportunity to make her savings bring a greater income,
such was the demand for money. Loan agents offered her an outlet. They agreed to make the loans,
make the mortgages and make collection, retaining
half the interest collected and returning the other
half with the principal to the possessor of the
money. For a time the business prospered.

Soon it was known that money on chattel security was available and the loan business perked up
satisfactorily. From four to six per cent a month
was the going interest charged, based upon the security offered and resisting power of the borrower.
An actual loan of this class typical of thousands
made during those trying periods was a loan of
$100 on three months' time. Six per cent a month
for three months on $100 would amount to $18.

This was deducted in advance and the borrower was given $82, and the $18 were divided between the loan agents and the owner of the money, and the deal was satisfactory to all parties.

The note signed by the borrower and his wife did not bear interest for three months but after maturity it bore both interest and penalty. To the inexperienced borrower, it looked fair to charge no interest and the accommodation of the money was well worth paying $18 for. The security was on a pair of horses, harness, lumber wagon and corn cultivator.

The sequel was the old, old story. The borrower was unable to pay the $100 note at the end of the three months. He was however able to raise another three months' interest or "penalty" to let the note run on. Then followed extensions, not renewals, and partial payments of penalty till finally the end and collapse came. The chattel security was surrendered and sold to satisfy the $100 note. The property proved to be in such a run down condition that horses, harness, wagon and corn plow only brought $25.50. The loan brokers had received half the interest as commission for their efforts. The borrower had returned a portion of the loan in interest and lost his farm team and equipment. The New England spinster had been paid some interest on her $100 saved from the dole of her meager earnings, and at the last received $25.50 for the $100 invested, less sale expenses.

A higher grade of money loaning became common as homesteaders made final proof on their claims and received government patents for their land. Typical of thousands of this class was the

homesteader who lived in poverty, without money,
without credit to buy farm equipment, struggling
along under great handicaps to the end of his five
years occupancy of his homestead, to learn that he
could postpone securing his land patent or accept
it and use it to secure a land loan of from $300 to
$500 at 10 per cent annual interest for five years.
As the state became older the amount of the loan
increased and interest grew less. Immediately the
homesteader was pressed by the merchant he owed,
or the energetic farm implement dealer to mortgage
his land. Added to these appeals the ambition to
buy a desirable pair of horses at a high price or
a few pigs or cows, was irresistible. The mortgage
was made. A Marsh harvester took most of the
loan. It never paid to own a harvester unless at
least 100 acres of grain was grown on the farm.
The homesteaders 25 acres was soon cut, and he
returned cutting grain for work he had swapped
with a neighbor, and the harvester was run into a
sun flower patch for shelter till next year. Two or
three years of this kind of shelter left the harvester
of little value and as the land had advanced in
value a heavier mortgage or a second or third
mortgage was laid to enable the homesteader to own
a newer harvester or more farm equipment. Then
the end came with the foreclosure of the mortgage
and eviction of the homesteader. It is estimated
that an average of two and a half settlers occupied
Nebraska homesteads before the one came that was
able to stay.

Great volumes could be written about the experiences of Nebraska sod house settlers similar to the
examples herewith given. They are typical, not in-

dividual experiences. Without the money loaners of the different clases it would have taken many more years to develop the country. The prolific .soil, the hard working settler, the privations of those who built up the state, would not have sufficed. The money loaners may have been extortionate, heartless, dishonest in some cases, but they took great risks. They helped develop the land. It may not be charged that they forced their extortionate interest on unwilling borrowers but the borrowers were eager to secure the loans.

CHAPTER XIX

The Sod House Doctor

"A Doctor's stock in trade consists
In looking wise and dam mysterious."
—*Josh Billings.*

HILE I was engaged in active practice of medicine a regrettable outbreak of sickness far from a doctor, was noted. A large family consisting of a widow and her grown up children by her two deceased husbands, filed claims on four quarter sections of land and built up a little village of sod houses and stables around the central surveyor's stake so each could live on his own homestead, yet all live near each other. They were a fine family of people, but happened to live 20 miles from any town where a doctor had located. Homesteaders were usually healthy but were subject to epidemics of diphtheria and typhoid fever because of unsanitary ways of living. This family developed a case of typhoid fever and a doctor was called from the town 20 miles distant on the south. He did not return for a second visit and the patient died. Another was attacked and a doctor from our town on the east was called. He was a good doctor but very slow and irregular in making his rounds. He failed to make a return call and his patient also died. Another was stricken, and my partner was called. Before time to make his second visit he went off on some political mission, and his patient took a relapse till he was at the point of death. Of course the survivors came after the doctor. Real-

izing the condition, I answered his call myself in time to view the corpse. I then assumed the responsibility of seeing them through the epidemic.

At the time, doctors realized that the unsanitary environments such as surrounded the sod houses, had something to do with spreading typhoid fever. I recognized that the number of people living close together was a feature, but medical knowledge did not yet connect flies as carriers in a typhoid epidemic. In this case there were no window or door screens and there was not a single out door toilet. The flies had an easy time to infect the entire family colony. I took that long 20 mile drive with a horse and buggy, making nearly twenty visits. The most of them had the fever in a form not as virulent as the first cases but I did not neglect them and no more deaths followed. When winter set in, the last patient was convalescing. At that time a doctor located within five miles of the colony and I turned my country hospital over to him.

Such experiences were common and the country doctor had to meet them. It was not wholly the fault of the sod houses that contagious diseases and epidemics were common. The common drinking cup, the open dug well, the outdoor toilet, or no toilet at all, shared the blame with the lack of ventilation and crowded quarters of the sod house. It was the same with the log cabin of the timber settler. Doctors and patients had not learned of the importance of preventive treatment and trusted wholly to internal medication when sickness laid its victim low, and trusted to luck when they were able to go about their business.

The floor of a dugout, or sod house, was commonly the clay dirt, innocent of joist or board flooring. It was not possible to scrub it or disinfect it of the millions of germs that found a breeding place in the dirt trodden under foot. Food in open dishes, milk, butter and the table dishes were easily contaminated with the germs raised in the dust if an attempt to sweep up the floor was attempted. The "no spitting" fad had not taken root and the wooden drinking pail in the corner held the supply of drinking water, and the drinking cup in common use went days at a time without being sterilized by boiling water. Disease germs were here, there, everywhere and anywhere. No wonder the mortality by diphtheria was so great among children and the old cemeteries tell the pathetic story of the wholesale slaughter of the innocents.

A country doctor related an experience he had with diphtheria in a typical early day, small sod house. A settler and his wife lived on their claim and were prospering. Both were young and strong and had two strong, young children. The father was obliged to absent himself from home two or three days marketing cattle. During his absence the children were both attacked with malignant diphtheria. On his return he brought them candy and in his pleasure at reaching home and love for the children, he gave them the little presents he had brought, and kissed them. The infection was contracted by the kisses and soon he was suffering in the grasp of a relentless foe with certain death in the near future. The fear of the disease kept visitors from the room where a malignant infection might be contracted, but the doctor did not desert the family. He informed them that death was imminent, although the mind of the sick man was clear. He advised that if the dying man desired to place his business affairs in order, to send to town at once for an attorney. The attorney not arriving, the doctor wrote down the wishes of the dying man on an old letter envelope and the dying statement of the husband and father was admitted to probate as his last will and testament.

The prevalence of contagious and infectious diseases among sod house pioneers may not be charged entirely to germs in the dust or lack of ventilation. Fleas and bedbugs infested the sod houses by the million. While those houses, as a rule, were warm in winter and fairly cool in summer for the human occupants, they favored fleas and bedbugs as well. Added to the lowering of vitality by lack of a balanced ration of food, proper preparation, lack of clothing and carelessness in exposures to drafts and changes of temperature, the wonder is not so much that disease and infection took a heavy toll, as the wonder that so many survived to spend their later lives in modern homes where the laws of ventilation, sanitation, heating, internal toilets and bath rooms replaced the half barbarous homes of the young settlers. Many of them were little more than children who had contracted life partnerships and emigrated to the new country where homes could be established by living on them. Many of the settlers were fresh from the Civil war and had not yet learned farming and the girls they married had not learned to be good housekeepers and none of them knew the laws of health required to withstand the hardships of sod house pioneering.

All ages were subject to contract diphtheria, but the young were more susceptible. What doctor can ever erase from his memory the picture of a young woman lying on a straw tick on a worn wooden bedstead, that shared with the table, stove and a few chairs, the furniture of a sod house room. The family rich in good land but impoverished in money and home or farm equipment. All ignorant of sickness, especially infectious diseases, sitting helpless while the life of a loved one was going out. The patient, with a diphtheria membrane stopping her breathing, her flesh spotted, discolored, blackened, putrid, rotting off while she lived. While perfectly conscious, not able to speak, but hungrily following the doctor's movement, her eyes fairly speaking, begging and beseeching him to afford her the relief that he was not able to give. Diphtheria antitoxin was unknown then.

The pioneer doctor saw many of those strong virile young people die perfectly conscious when in an older country an aged person would be blessed by a curtain of unconsciousness that permitted the sufferer to fall gently to sleep. Compare with the next century with its luxurious homes or modern hospitals with all comforts and trained nurses in charge and then do not attempt to deny honor and glory to the pioneers who went through sickness, poverty, exposure and privation that their descendants might live in comfort or even luxury.

Maternity came often to those sod houses and because of the age of the settlers, large families were common. It came in obedience to the natural laws of descent, while many kinds of sickness came because of disobedience to the laws of health. Noth-

ing else did so much for the upbuilding of the state.
Without those troops of boys and girls the prairies
of Nebraska would have been barren wastes and
the sod house homes but dreams. The sacred privacy of maternity in those crowded sod houses
must not be opened to the vulgar gaze of the public. A hurried exchange of a family of children to
a neighbor's house, and the return of one or more
women to the home they had left and if a doctor
was available, a drive or horseback ride to a distant
town and the subsequent report of the arrival of
a new citizen would be announced. For a few days
the children or the father, possibly helped by a
neighbor woman, prepared the family food. The
washing was taken to a neighbors. As soon as old
enough, the district school grew larger by one
scholar.

But maternity did not always pass so happily.
I know a doctor who could tell of a call where the
wife was well advanced in years when married.
After two days it could not be denied that her life
or her child's life must be lost. Craniotomy and a
birth in dismembered pieces, limb by limb, skull in
pieces, that the mother might live. Or a careless
doctor ignorant of modern sterilizing processes,
carried infection to a mother who left her family
by the child bed-fever route.

Sometimes the settler must depend upon the country surgeon to relieve a serious injury. A call to
take a thirty mile drive with a horse and buggy on a
hot summer day to try to save the life of a farmer
who had slipped off a hay stack onto the big wood-
en handle of a pitchfork that entered his body. Or
a strong pioneer dying in his sod house while under-

going an operation for bladder calculi at the hands of an inexperienced doctor, assisted by a common druggist. The doctor, who had braced his nerve for the ordeal by liberal libations of spiritus frumenti, failed to cease operating for sometime after his patient had died.

Then in the infancy of appendectomy two country doctors while trying to save a young settler's life by performing an operation they did not understand, accidentally cut into a neighboring organ. Modern surgery makes light of such incisions but they thought that they had given a fatal wound so closed the incision and let the patient die a natural death from appendicitis.

Or the amusing thing of the small son of a distinctly Irish mother being bitten on the bulbous part of his anatomy by a dog that collected a liberal size morsel for his own use. Then the gathering of an excited, superstitious mob of sympathizers, who believed that a person who had been bitten by a dog would suffer from hydrophobia should the dog at any future time, no matter how remote, suffer from hydrophobia. The only certain protection for the bitten boy was the death of the dog before he had a chance to contract the disease.

A sod house settler who had been engaged in heavy lifting work all day was acutely attacked with great pain and his condition was so alarming that he thought death was imminent. A man on a horse was sent post haste for a doctor. No one knew what the man was suffering from but the customary hot packs and mustary poultices were freely applied. The doctor arrived and diagnosed strangulated hernia. He failed to reduce it by manipulation and sent for another doctor to help him. By that time the gravity of the case brought a congregation of sympathetic neighbors who feared their friend was passing. The use of chloroform and other relaxants did not permit the hernia to be reduced. It was decided to call a surgeon from a distant town to operate.

The surgeon arrived, and the neighbors in their sympathy got gloriously lit up and would go and look on their friend and then rush out weeping drunken tears copiously, and take another drink. The surgeon thought to try another relaxant before using the knife. A druggist was employed to make a tobacco decoction. Understanding his business he got all the strength out of a quarter pound of fine cut tobacco and this was used as a rectal injection. It certainly caused a relaxation but for hours the patient laid at the point of death. The visiting surgeon was not able to rally him and reluctantly retired while the local doctor spent all night following the tobacco decoction with brandy injections. Consciousness and heart action returned after several hours' efforts and the operation was performed the next day.

There were no dentists in the sod house country and the doctors extracted the aching teeth. My partner became famous as a tooth extractor. Sometimes he brought liberal helpings of jaw bone. One day a man came in complaining that a small hole in a big molar distracted him with pain and he desired its removal. The doctor was expeditious but mistook the tooth and extracted the sound molar on the other side.

The ingenuity of the settlers in pursuit of brandy and whiskey made the country doctor much trouble. They wanted prescriptions containing whiskey or brandy for warding off both heat and cold, for chills and for fever, and for snake bites, but mostly because they wanted it. He imagined a pain in his "tummy" called for blackberry brandy with ginger and most anything else only the blackberry must be plentiful. Once I was appealed to, to cure a severe attack of abdominal pain by a big fat barber who named his drugs all to be smothered in brandy. I told him he could have the drugs but he would have to forego the brandy and take it in water. This he refused to do and departed with his stomach pains. For years he made a stock story of my inhumanity to man, explaining the circumstances. Finally he rehearsed it to an elderly clerical gentleman. I explained the circumstances and reminded the old gentleman of the barber's generous waist girth and red face, and inquired if in his opinion I was not justified in keeping the barber out of the way of temptation by withholding brandy, and giving the medicine in water. The decision came quickly: "Ah, Mr. Jonsing vas right. One drop brandy more vort than two barrels of vater."

CHAPTER XX

Grand Army of the Republic

"We pledge allegiance to the Flag of the United States of America and the People for which it stands; One Nation, Indivisible, with liberty and justice for all."

N0 CLASS of people exerted a more dominating influence in developing Nebraska during the formative period of the first thirty years of statehood than did the survivors of the American Civil war. Nearly three millions of the young men of the North had been enrolled as soldiers in that great internal strife. Probably, excluding re-enlistments and rejections because of disabilities, two and a half million were inducted into the service of the North and while there is no dependable record, no doubt two millions of the young men of the South served in the Confederate armies.

Of the millions of volunteer soldiers, mostly boys in their teens, a great many were under 18 years of age when they took service in the armies of both Federal and Confederate armies. They were officered and led by older men. Many of the officers were prominent in affairs at home, but knew little about military tactics or military affairs. Naturally, professional men, lawyers, doctors, educators and ministers became commanding officers till in time the few educated soldiers, who had been taught the art of war at the West Point Military Academy, became leaders. With them came men and officers who had belonged to military organizations or independent companies during peace times and thus gained a smattering of the duties of camp and field. There were also many men who attained leadership who had been given military training in Europe. As a rule, it was West Point graduates who came to be the supreme leaders of the victorious armies, but there were many prominent officers who had their start in independent military companies. General Miles was such an officer and eventually became commander-in-chief of the armies of the United States. There were many educated officers in the southern states where the leisure class turned to military affairs more than civilians in the northern states did.

At the time of the Civil war the country was agricultural and the armies of the North were largely made up of country boys who had scarcely ever been off the farm. Transportation was slow and travel seldom thought of. The most of those boys had not advanced in school studies beyond the sixth grade. They had been educated to work and those from the middle west had learned to shoot. Efficiently led, they made excellent soldiers. The boys from the South who entered the Confederate service, and along the border divided between both armies, were equally qualified as marksmen and equally brave but had been subordinated by slavery curse and had not been trained to hard work. But there were educated officers in the South to train and lead them in war.

Those millions of boys who went to war learned that they need not linger around the home where their forbears had been raised. They imbibed the spirit of wanderlust during the four years of active service in the army that took them to new places they would not have thought of visiting had not the army service required it. Leaving home as young school boys, they were mustered out of the service as determined, world-wise young men with life before them. From timid, shrinking country boys, lacking resolution to strike out into the world for themselves, they had developed into forceful, vigorous, combative strong men. During their years in service, they had learned self-reliance and the democracy of the volunteer army made them equal with their officers, many of whom had grown up with them at home.

The great prairies of the territories and newly made states beckoned for the brawn and brain of the mustered out soldiers of the Civil war. They had learned the spirit of adventure in the armies of Tennessee and Virginia. The home nest was too small and environments too constricted for them to endure. The best education they had gained during their military service was self reliance and that opportunity waited those who would spread their wings and fly. They were ready and soon they were swarming to Nebraska and Kansas where free homes waited them where the soil was fertile and the climate congenial. The girls of the period were ready to accompany them and the westward trek saw few boys in blue leaving "The girl I left behind me."

It is safe to say that no state in the union contained a larger percentage of Civil war veterans than Nebraska did during the thirty-year period following its admission to the union of states. The faded blue left from the service uniform and the bronze emblem of membership in the G. A. R. Post was in evidence everywhere. No class of men exerted as profound an influence in developing Nebraska and directing its policies as did the boys in blue. Everywhere they were the dominating influence. In progressive movements for better schools, better homes, transportation, legislation, the professions, and in fact everywhere ex-service men were the ruling influence. The freedom from home restraint and independent action that were learned during their absence in the service and carried the boys to victory in war was equally potent to carry them to victory in civil affairs and to over come obstacles nature had placed between them and the prosperous homes they sought to establish in Nebraska. Added to the thousands of Civil war soldiers who went into the service from the territory of Nebraska, and returned after they were mustered out, came untold thousands from the eastern states. The developing of the state of Nebraska was dominated and directed by the legions of the nation who had been matured in the great fraternal war of the country.

The hardships of camp and field had prepared them for the hardships of pioneer life. They all brought youth and hope, but not all came through the ordeals of war retaining their full health. Many broke down in health prematurely, but to a greater or lesser degree, helped form and direct the ship of state into a safe harbor. They were the rank and file and a large part of the flesh, blood and sinew that went to make the composite citizen of the prairie of the middle west.

A Douglas political cartoon used in the campaign of 1860. Negro slavery contentions brought secession of southern states and the civil war

Prize Winners at County Fair.

As a member of an U. S. Pension Examining
Board I participated in the examination of four
hundred disabled Civil war veterans. I asked the
questions to gain their story, wrote their disabilities
into the record and forwarded a copy of the U. S.
Pension Department. It was in this way that I
gained much information about the hardships of
homesteading the prairies of Nebraska that aggra-
vated greatly the disabilities incurred in the service
of their country.

Besides taking a full part in subduing the prairies, establishing schools and churches, building
prosperous homes, accomplishing needed laws and
upholding courts in enforcing the laws, they were
the moving spirit that taught loyalty to country and
honor to the flag of the country to the boys and
girls in the public schools. It was they who brought
the stars and stripes to the assembled pupils and
taught the children the flag salute. When war came
later it was always the Civil war veterans who led
in the honors and gave God speed to the departing
soldiers as they themselves had been given God-
speed when they answered the call to fight for the
preservation of the Union.

The Grand Army of the Republic was the organization they rallied around and their wives, mothers,
daughters and sisters did service in the Woman's
Relief Corps. Early in 1866 the Grand Army of
the Republic was organized in the older states. Requirements for membership were service in the
army, navy or marine corps between April 12, 1861,
and April 9, 1865. Service alone was not all. An
honorable discharge was required and no one could

be accepted who had, at anytime, borne arms against the United States.

An organization of the G. A. R. in Nebraska was attempted in 1867 but was abandoned. A permanent department was organized in 1877 and annual encampments and annual reunions were held and only abandoned when age and disease sounded taps for the survivors. To the Sons of Veterans they gave over their work and the W. R. C. relinquished their activities to the Daughters of Veterans.

The objects sought to be accomplished by the organization of soldiers who saw service under the stars and stripes during the Civil war, were stated as follows:

To secure the passage of laws favorable to the soldiers, their wives and dependent children. Homes for disabled and helpless veterans. Homes for dependent soldiers and families and hospitals for their care were established. Burial of veterans and tomb stones were provided for. In 1889 state legislation was carried to provide a tax of three-tenths of a mill on all property to raise a fund to be devoted to the relief of honorably discharged soldiers and their families and the appointment of three residents of each county called "The Soldiers' Relief Commission" to disburse this fund. These were but a few of the things the Grand Army of the Republic working as a body accomplished.

Nebraska was essentially a soldier state. But most of the accomplishments of the former soldiers were done as citizens of the state and their work was done as individuals rather than by organization. Building of sod house homes, breaking the wild prairies, planting, reaping and marketing, establishing churches and schools and suffering all the hardships, labor and joys of a homesteaders life they took their full part. They saw sickness, death and sorrow. They endured disappointment and became feeble from their labors. They established law and order and fought Indians and poverty but they never flinched.

The Grand Army of the Republic is an honorable name. In war its members saved the union of states and obliterated the curse of slavery. In peace they led in warfare against ignorance, irreligion, crime, and promoted loyalty and industry and taught obedience to law. Their bodies molder in the dust but their services to civilization and humanity will never die.

CHAPTER XXI

Evolution of the Nebraska National Guard

*"Millions for defense, but not one cent
for tribute."—Pinckney.*
*"For if the trumpet give an uncertain
sound, who shall prepare himself to
the battle."—First Corinthians.*

HE National Guard of the states is the
offspring of the colonial militia and the
militia men of the early days of the federated states. "Militia," is derived from
military, and means a body of soldiers.
Soon after the colonies became federated
into the United States of America, the
necessity of having a system for calling a body of
armed men for protection against the Indians was
apparent. The custom had been to call for volunteers
to repel desultory attacks of Indians or make predatory or punitive expeditions against them when
they became troublesome. Such bodies of fighting
men were hardly to be classed as military, because
they lacked organization and were not led by law-
fully constituted officers. Naturally, such men
chafed at discipline, yet might be valiant fighters.

The matter of providing a more orderly way of
conducting expeditions of offense and providing for
defense was considered by the federal congress in
1797. Some of the colonies, notably Virginia, had
organized militia companies for years prior to the
war of Independence that had done effective service. The United States congress passed a militia

law in 1797 that provided that all able bodied men between the ages of 18 and 45 were constituted a part of the militia. They were required to equip themselves with a musket, a horn of powder, three gun flints and sixteen leaden bullets, each weighing an ounce. Under this law, or state laws of their own, some of the New England states and New York state instituted militia laws that required a training day mobilization at a designated point, at least once a year. The meeting might last two or three days and a sort of loose organization might or might not be formed with officers elected from among their number. It was in most cases a farce.

Training day meetings had more of a social than military character. Under the inspiration of corn whiskey, fights and grudges of long standing were settled. Neighborhoods determined athletic claims of superiority. A neighborhood would put out as its champion the best wrestler, the best runner, best jumper or best rifle shot and the championship was settled while military training languished. However, some militia companies organized and elected efficient officers and took pride in their uniform and equipment and social organization. My father belonged to such a rifle company in New York state. They were uniformed in dark green fringed hunting shirts with a cap having a brass military device rising aloft instead of the military cockade. Their equipment consisted of a flint lock rifle, ammunition pouch, leaden bullets and powder horn. Auxiliary to this was a scalping knife and tomahawk held in the belt. The inspiration for this make up came from the Green Mountain riflemen of Vermont in revolutionary war times. They ignored ordinary

drill, but practiced Indian methods of fighting. They
became expert riflemen, shooting at a mark standing, kneeling or lying flat on the ground. The
charging process of a muzzle loader and the powder
pan of a flint lock gun was tedious. To avoid exposure to gun fire from lurking Indians, loading was
practiced lying flat on the back.

As a rule the drill on training day began with
taking the marching step behind a fife and drum
band for a short time, then firing a salvo from such
guns as could be induced to explode gun powder.
Only a few had guns. Soon these were stacked and
the main events of the day took place to settle the
dispute as to which neighborhood could produce the
best man. Sometimes it was a dirty fight in which
all modern ring rules were ignored. Biting, kicking, gouging were allowed and no fouls considered.
The most popular contest was wrestling. This was
the "square hold" or catch as catch can. My mother
had a brother who qualified as a champion wrestler.
On one training day, another neighborhood put forward a negro wrestler as their champion to chal-
lenge all comers to a test of skill. Uncle said he
would never back from a "stump," even if it was a
black one. They went to the mat, or rather the
barn floor, and the colored man was thrown so vio-
lently that he died from a broken neck.

The National Militia law held for over 100 years
without change. In time it became apparent that to
call a citizen soldiery, seldom called to drill, lacking
in discipline and education, "Soldiers," was a mis-
nomer. The name "Guard" was deemed to be more
appropriate. National Guards were authorized by

most states before the obsolete federal militia law of 1797 was repealed. The militia held that they were not subject to be called to service outside their own states and, as a rule, refused to obey orders that called them to cross a state line or national border line into another country. An instance of such refusal occured during the war of 1812. A small body of U. S. troops crossed the Niagara river below the falls and captured the Queentown Height fort and killed General Brock, a celebrated British officer. The American leader recrossed the Niagara river to bring over his supporting force of New York militia to hold the fort his handful of regular soldiers had taken, but the militia absolutely refused to cross the river and go outside the state of New York. Noting this, the British rallied and drove the American regulars into the river and regained their lost fort.

Nebraska territory followed the old time custom of fighting Indians. It was done by individuals or by volunteers joining a group as the whites had done since the beginning of the occupancy of America. Two regiments of splendid soldiers were recruited in Nebraska territory during the Civil war. The First Nebraska Volunteers did valiant service in the Army of the Tennessee under General Grant. It was commanded by General John M. Thayer who afterward became governor of Nebraska. The Second Nebraska was kept in the territory to protect the citizens against uprisings of the Indians and their depredations on the settlers. Those regiments were in no way connected with the state militia or the later National Guards. They were recruited and inducted into the service of the

United States as U. S. Volunteers and discharged from service as such.

The first act of the Nebraska legislature leading to military organization was made by the second territorial legislature that met in 1858. Nebraska territorial fighting men made a wonderful record fighting Indians by volunteer companies and the organized companies enlisted for that purpose. The record of the First Nebraska during the Civil war was a brilliant one and many Nebraskans saw service in Kansas or Iowa regiments. Nebraska settlers successfully established a record for fighting and on that foundation the Nebraska National Guard was finally developed.

The Nebraska legislature in 1881 repealed existing militia laws and established the Nebraska National Guard and designated its name. This was the beginning of the Nebraska National Guard. The act provided for a force not exceeding 2,000 men and prescribed an oath of allegiance and that the organization, discipline and system of exercises, must conform to those of the United States army. Under the commander-in-chief, the governor of the state, the duties of the National Guard were to execute the law, suppress insurrection or repel invasion, and upon requisition by the president of the United States, and proclamation by the governor, under certain conditions, be enrolled to do service outside the state.

The staff of the commander-in-chief consisted of an adjutant general with the rank of brigadier general, a quartermaster general and a surgeon general each with the rank of colonel. An inspector general with the rank of lieutenant colonel, a judge advocate general with rank of major and as many staff aids as he may think proper to appoint. The duties of the staff aids were personal and social. The adjutant general, commissary general and surgeon general were charged with the purchase of the supplies required in their departments and have command over their departments, under the commander-in-chief. The surgeon general by virtue of his position became chief surgeon of the National Guard. His duties were partly to examine and approve surgeons for the brigade and regiments and hold supreme command over members of his department under the governor. He ranked all medical officers of the Guard. The adjutant general ranked all officers of the Guard and had supreme command, under the governor, over all combat troops.

The National Guard act provided for the supply of uniforms and equipment for the enlisted men and one dollar a day pay when in actual service. Officers, when on duty, were to receive pay equalling the pay of officers of the same rank in the United States service.

Following the National Guard legislative act, two regiments of infantry of 12 companies each, designated as First and Second Regiments, a cavalry troop and an artillery company were organized. The companies were formed in different towns of the state and might be mobilized at some convenient locality in the state for instruction. The eighties were active in organization but the Guard was not called on for notable service. Early during the nineties a substantial part of the Guard was called to South Omaha to preserve peace during a labor strike but the services required of them was little more than to act as a moral support to the civil authorities.

Early in 1891 the Nebraska National Guard was mobilized along the northern part of Nebraska between Chadron and Valentine to protect the settlers from an outbreak of hostile Indians. The settlers feared a repetition of the murders of white people in Minnesota in 1862 when the Indians, taking advantage of the diversion of men to the Civil war battle-fields, attacked and destroyed many settlements and killed and wounded hundreds of white people. The Nebraska National Guard had the honor of participating in this the last decisive campaign against hostile Indians who retained tribal relations. This campaign closed several hundred years of warfare with native red men who contested the advance of civilization step by step.

Beginning on the Atlantic coast the struggles between the Indians and the whites had been a continuous affair. Murders of isolated settlers by marauding Indians were numerous. Armed bodies of whites sent against them were sometimes successful, and sometimes suffered defeat. National history gives the winning of the states north of the Ohio river and south of the Great Lakes the most prominent place in Indian warfare, but the greatest and swiftest movements, the greatest campaigns and a great part of Indian warfare occurred west of the Missouri river. These contacts were located so far from the centers of population and civilization, that American history has never given the Indian warfare on the plains and mountains the place in the history of accomplishments it deserves.

Beginning with the occupancy of Nebraska and Kansas, a thirty year Indian war followed filled with victories and defeat for both sides. Nebraska was the center of a continuous battle-field. Nature could not stop the eviction of the Indian and buffalo from the fertile lands they claimed. Indians were at times mistreated, robbed and suffered injustice and much of the dealings with them was vacillating and dishonest and encouraged the worst members of the numerous tribes to think that the whites were afraid of them. The U. S. West Point Military Academy sent their graduates to the plains to fight Indians to complete their training. Frequent expeditions were sent against hostile Indians. Several detachments of soldiers were completely destroyed. Notably the celebrated cavalry soldier, General Custer and the major part of the Seventh cavalry, were killed to a man by the hostile Indians in Montana.

Late in the eighties Gen. Miles, fresh from the conquest of the Arizona Apache Indians, was in command of the U. S. troops guarding against the hostile Indians in South Dakota and trying to round them up at the agencies. January 1, 1891, about 20,000 Sioux Indians were located in the neighborhood of Pine Ridge Agency situated on the line between Nebraska and South Dakota. About 8,000 U. S. soldiers were endeavoring to keep them peaceful. Among this force was the reorganized Seventh U. S. cavalry including a few of the survivors who were in the detachment that escaped the massacre by the Indians. Inflamed by their medicine men, 4,000 of those Indians were trying to escape and go on the war-path. Indian police from the agency in trying to arrest the ruling chief, Sitting Bull, had a fight in which Sitting Bull, and several Indians and police were killed. Several killings had occurred and the settlers of northern Nebraska were mindful of the Indian outbreak in Minnesota in 1862 in which the country was overrun by the outlaw Indians and hundreds of citizens murdered. The Minnesota outbreak was checked, and an example made by executing 38 Indians together at a public hanging.

At this time the Nebraska National Guard did the most noteworthy service in its history. The Nebraska settlers were wild with fear and excitement and were pleading with the governor for protection, and many left their homes and fled for safety. Victor Vifquain, was adjutant general of the Nebraska National Guard and a distinguished veteran of the Civil war. By directions of the governor, he ordered the Nebraska Brigade of National Guard under Brigadier General Colby to mobilize at once along the war zone and relieve the regular soldiers of the task of guarding the white settlers. This he did admirably and his disposition of his command met the approval of General Miles. General headquarters with supply depots and regimental headquarters were established and detachments placed in towns at strategetic points over the entire territory between Valentine and Chadron, and ranches were occupied by National Guard companies as fortified outposts.

For some time prior to the calling of the Nebraska National Guard to support the U. S. regular troops by protecting the settlers in northern Nebraska, the thousands of Indians who roamed over the unoccupied lands of the Dakotas, Wyoming and Montana, and as the mood visited them crossed the border into Canada, had been in a dangerous state of unrest. A part of them were willing to settle down around the Indian agencies but many of them were irreconcilables and determined on a war to exterminate the white people. They had to be constantly watched to keep them from going on the war path. They were incited to warfare by their medicine men at religious meetings they staged far from the agencies where they engaged in "ghost dances" as their alleged religious meetings were called in which their worship consisted of a wild dance in which they became excited to a frenzy by their medicine men. They were told that the "ghost shirts" they were induced to wear could not be penetrated by the bullets of the soldiers. It required thousands of soldiers and the help of the Indian police to subdue the many outbreaks and prevent a general uprising.

It was at this period that a band of 340 of the most dangerous of the irreconcilables were gathered together at Wounded Knee creek and guarded by the Seventh U. S. Cavalry. It was sought to disarm the Indians and one morning they were all ordered to assemble outside their teepees and give up their arms. They only surrendered a few worthless weapons. Thereupon a search of the teepees was made by the soldiers and many good weapons were found. All the time the medicine man was going among them inciting them to resistance assuring them that they were safe because the bullets of the soldiers would not penetrate their shirts. Finally an Indian drew a gun from under his blanket and fired at the soldiers and immediately the fight was on. The Indians had knives and revolvers hidden under their blankets but soon the fight became a massacre, only this time the Seventh cavalry was victorious. A blood insanity seemed to have possessed them and the soldiers killed men, women, and children indiscriminately. The result was that 220 Indians and 31 soldiers lost their lives besides those who died of wounds, some of the wounded lay on the ground in the snow four days before being relieved.

The fight degenerated into a massacre such as the Indians always dealt the whites under like conditions. Revenge may have instigated the cavalry to kill, when the fighting ceased. It may have been cruel and wasteful of life but the bloody result and severe punishment completely subdued the Indians and it was the turning point of the hundreds of years of warfare and Indian resistance to the whites. One member of the Nebraska Guard and a cattle herder lost their lives in the fight. Another fight followed at the same place a few days later in which a supply train was attacked by a body of Indians and repulsed. The end of Indian warfare came with the Wounded Knee engagement and the very severity of the punishment seemed to have subdued the Indians for all time. In this last of the conflicts between Indians under tribal rule and organized military, the Nebraska National Guard had an honorable part by relieving the regular soldiers of guarding the lives of non-combatants. While they stood ready to engage in actual combat should their services be needed, their services, in acting as a reserve force for the regular army, gave them the honor of engaging in the last Indian campaign that began nearly 300 years before when the races were striving for supremacy. They were upholding the flag of their country and of civilization when the final armistice between savagery and civilization was ended by the severe and bloody punishment meted out to the last of the irreconcilable hostile Indians at Wounded Knee.

In reporting the campaign to his commander-in-chief, General Colby illustrated by a military map showing the distribution and assignment of his troops that is an interesting study and demonstrated his competency.

CHAPTER XXII

Nebraska National Guard in Action

"Where'er you go,
You know, friend or foe,
Receive the hand or toe
Of the bold soger boy."
—*Old Song*

T HE Guard organization was kept up and improved till the Spanish war was declared in 1898. Then the Nebraska National Guard volunteered its services subject to the call of the President of the United States, agreeable to the laws of Nebraska. The offer was accepted and Secretary of War, Russel Alger, informed them that it was the wish of President McKinley to use the National Guards as much as possible because they were already armed, equipped and drilled. Two Nebraska regiments responded to the call of the President dated April 23, 1898. Mobilization of the Nebraska Guard was at the state fair grounds at Lincoln.

Lieutenant Stotsenburg, of the Sixth U. S. Cavalry, had been detailed as military instructor at the University of Nebraska and occupied the position of commandant of the university cadets. He was assigned to the First Nebraska Infantry as senior major. Two calls were made by the President totalling 3,382 men based on the census reports. The strength of the Nebraska National Guard as provided by Nebraska law must not exceed 2,000 men. In all, the state furnished 4,016 men divided between the First, Second and Third Infantry and Troop "K" of the Third U. S. Cavalry.

The First Nebraska under Col. John Bratt was entrained for service in the Philippines. The Second Nebraska under Col. William Bischof was sent to the Chickamauga Park, Civil war battle-field, in northern Georgia and there held in camp till the close of the war. Their suffering from sickness and typhoid fever was appalling. The First Nebraska entered Manila Bay after the destruction of the Spanish fleet by Admiral Dewey and participated in the capture of the city. This was accomplished with the loss of one private of the First Nebraska, killed, and several wounded. The capture of the city of Manila was followed by the close of the Spanish war.

The Third Nebraska was inducted into the service under the second call, but was not, properly speaking, a unit of the National Guard. W. J. Bryan was commissioned Colonel. They saw no active service in the field.

The First Nebraska National Guard, as the First Nebraska U. S. V. Infantry, did wonderful service in subduing the insurrection of the natives in the Philippines. It was a much more formidable affair to pacify the natives than it was to displace the Spanish land troops from the Philippines, or from Cuba. In the long campaign, the First Nebraska was at the long end of the forward march that circled through the country while the other end remained fixed at Manila. The pen has been declared mightier than the sword, and the pen of reporters failed to give the First Nebraska the credit for deeds they did, as much as they did the 20th Kansas with its spectacular Colonel Funston who was a gallant soldier of fortune. Col. Bills had resigned the command of the First Nebraska after the close of the war with the Spaniards and Major Stotsenburg had been made Colonel by the governor of Nebraska. He was a finished soldier, a graduate of West Point and would have ranked Col. Funston after the war. By the irony of fate, his death was probably all that prevented him from occupying the position Pershing held during the world war. Pershing succeeded Funston after the latters death during the expedition into Mexico, and was sent to France as supreme commander with the first detail of U. S. troops. Both Pershing and Stotsenburg were West Point graduates and both had been Commandants and military instructors at the University of Nebraska.

After the surrender of Manila some of the First Nebraska men thinking that the war was over, wanted to go home. They were stationed in the city at first, and dissatisfied members began to send home complaints against the discipline Colonel Stotsenburg had supplanted for the lack of discipline in the city. They were moved out into the country and Stotsenburg soon made the regiment into the best fighting regiment on the Island. To the shame of the Nebraska legislature be it said that they listened to the complaints sent home by a few "pets" and passed resolutions censuring Colonel Stotsenburg in a way that would have discredited a scolding fishwife. An investigation followed and a long list of the findings was included in General Barry's report of 1899-1900 completely exonerating

Col. Stotsenburg. Once in the field the men realized what the Colonel had done for them and no leader was ever more popular than he was.

The first shot of the insurrection was fired by a First Nebraska sentinel on guard at the camp where the regiment held the most distant outpost. They started the war and continued till they finished. They were opposed by natives armed with all kinds of weapons. The chance for a sentinel to be struck by an arrow while walking his beat in the dark was not enticing to a citizen soldier. At the battle where Col. Stotsenburg was killed, Lieutenant Sisson of "K" company was also killed. Both were shot through the heart apparently by a sharpshooter as they stood close together.

I have a volume of radiograph pictures illustrating gunshot wounds received during the Spanish war. They were taken from X-ray pictures and prepared by the Medical Department of the United States illustrating the location of missiles by the Rontgen Ray process. Two gunshot wounds so chosen for illustration were received by members of the First Nebraska.

One picture shows a Mauser bullet plainly outlined in the brain of Private John Gretner of "D" company. The bullet had struck him in his forehead just to left of center and above his left eye. He so far recovered that he entered the mail service after his discharge from the hospital and returned to the Philippines.

The other was Cornelius Fagan. He was raised in Boone county and enlisted as a private in "K" company at Columbus. In the attack on Block House No. 7, the next day after the war with the natives started, he was struck over the left eye by a .45 Remington bullet. It passed through his head destroying the sight of his right eye and lodged in his face where the X-ray shows it in the antrum on right side. Two operations were necessary to remove the missile. His subsequent history was that he died some years after his discharge from the hospital. It was understood that the wound was a contributing cause of death.

Some of the natives were savages and had no knowledge of civilized war weapons. The U. S. troops were equipped with those small portable howitzers that were carried on a mule. They were effective in throwing shells and made a big noise. One native said he could understand the noise of the gun but not the explosion of the shell at a distance. In his words, "Me sabe ze zoom," pointing to the gun, "but me no sabe ze zoom, zoom," pointing first at the gun and then where the shell exploded in the distance.

The records show that no detachment of American troops accomplished more than the First Nebraska during the insurrection of natives in the Philippines, not excluding the regular soldiers. No regiment, national guard or regular troops, suffered the casualties, killed in battle, that the Nebraska First did. The 20th Kansas was a close second, but because of their spectacular little Colonel Funston, they got a great deal of publicity. The records show that the First Nebraska lost, killed in action, 23 and, died of wounds, 15, making a total loss in action, 38. They also lost by typhoid fever, 13, and including other causes a total death loss of 65. The 20th Kansas lost in action, 17, died of wounds, 17, making a total of 34. Instead of losing heavily by typhoid they lost 13 by smallpox and a total death loss of 58.

In mentioning the activities of the First Nebraska U. S. Volunteers in the Philippines, it must be recalled that the service was different from the service of the First Nebraska U. S. V. during the Civil war when the men were enlisted directly for service in response to the call of President Lincoln for Volunteers. President McKinley called the First and Second Nebraska to service as National Guards, under a Nebraska law, and they at no time ceased to be under the supervision of the governor of Nebraska. Only their movements in the field were commanded by United States military authorities who ranked above Colonel. Discharges for disability came from the regimental or state authorities. Promotion of officers came from the governor of Nebraska. Thus it came that Major Stotsenburg was advanced over Lieutenant Colonel Cotton to the colonelcy when Col. Bratt resigned. At home, Captain Killian of K company was a political opponent of the governor who recognized him as a competent officer and advanced him to the position of major. The services of the First Nebraska in the Spanish war was that of a National Guard regiment beginning with the agitation of threatened war early in 1897 and continued till the return of the regiment in 1899. It was mustered out in California, but the men were returned to Nebraska on a special train paid for by citizens of the state and were given a reception in Omaha, and later one in Lincoln, when at a formal reception on the state house grounds, Colonel Mulford, who had succeeded to the colonelcy, delivered up the flag of the regiment in an appropriate address. It was responded to by Gov. Poynter, who was in the band stand where he was surrounded by notables, including the assistant secretary of war, Meikeljohn, and National Guard staff officers.

The call of the National Guard regiments to arms and induction into the volunteer service of the United States occurred during Governor Holcomb's administration. It was volunteering by National Guard regiments rather than individuals. The First and Second regiments, N. N. G., were inducted into the service at the first call. The Second Regiment, equally anxious to engage in combat as the First Regiment, was unfortunate from the first. It was mobilized and sent to Chickamauga Park, in northern Georgia, where the men suffered severely from typhoid fever and were never active in service. The Third Nebraska that volunteered under the second call of the President, was sent to Georgia and later to Cuba but saw no actual service because the Spanish war was over. Not a single National Guard, officer or private, and not a particle of supplies, equipment, arms, ammunition, army or medical supplies remained in Nebraska.

William A. Poynter took the oath of office as Governor of Nebraska in January, 1899. The unsettled condition of the world threatened war. The ease with which the United States armies defeated the land forces of Spain and the thoroughness with which our navy destroyed the Spanish fleets, amazed the world to find that the United States had suddenly become the dominating world power. Germany only discovered that fact twenty years later.

The world was unsettled and the Boxer uprising and war with China imminent. The hardest part of the Spanish war, the insurrection of the natives of the Philippines was yet to come. It was the plain duty of Governor Poynter to reorganize the National Guard and prepare it for service in other wars that the unsettled condition of the world might bring about. Captain Patrick H. Barry, a veteran of the Civil war had served as adjutant general of the Guard under Gov. Holcomb, who inducted the Guard regiments into the service of the general government, had seen all the state supplies disappear with the men when they entered the U. S. service. He was reappointed to the same position by Gov. Poynter. Captain Barry had a fine Civil war record and had lost an arm in battle. He was well educated in military tactics and customs, a well poised man of good judgment and had himself under control at all times. He was a strict disciplinarian and a stickler for observing details, and a persistent worker. It fell to him to begin at once the reorganization of the Guard.

When Mr. Poynter became governor he found the First Nebraska National Guard Regiment in the Philippines and the Spanish war at an end. The insurrection of the natives was yet to come and would be a much more formidable conflict than with the Spanish troops. At the close of Spanish hostilities the Second Nebraska had been mustered out of the service and the Third Nebraska was doing guard duty in Cuba.

Gov. Poynter was an old acquaintance of mine and we had been associated in various community enterprises together. He invited me to accept the position of surgeon general on his headquarters staff and undertake the organization of the medical department, which under the existing conditions, and the law, carried much responsibility.

Under the law at the time Gen. Barry was given charge of organization and securing supplies and directing movements of combat troops and I was given the same authority for equipping and organizing the medical department. The governor never interfered with my administration in the least but approved of my expenditures of State funds for surgical and medical equipment and medical supplies.

Early in 1899 Gen. Barry began organizing companies in different towns to become members of the new Second Nebraska National Guard Regiment. He drew heavily on the U. S. government for supplies and equipment. The cavalry troop was organized and a regimental band joined to the Second regiment. The new Guard began to rise from the ashes of the one swallowed up in the Spanish war. A very successful encampment, or school of instruction, was held at the Epworth Park and driving association grounds near Lincoln in September, 1899.

During my incumbency of the office, in which I served two years as the chief medical officer of the Nebraska National Guard, I established headquarters and hospitals with dispensing tents at encampments. I served on many details and boards. I approved medical officers and gave officers of the Guard physical examinations. I sometimes rode a stiff livery horse, wearing my service uniform in a parade participated in by the governor and his staff aids.

The U. S. government was requisitioned for stretchers. Gen. Barry produced the tents and camp cots for the hospital from somewhere. I bought a brigade medical campaign chest for the brigade and one for each of the regiments. I also supplied surgical cases with instruments for use of the surgeons of each unit. Two orderly pouches for each company containing first aid supplies, including service knife, were bought and issued.

At camps of instruction I attended the officers meeting and urged that a detail be made from each company to be taught stretcher drill and first aid methods. I requested that drug clerks or medical students be preferred, rather than the customary detail of those who could not keep step in march or learn the drill. These men reported and were given instructions and the start so given grew into the organization of a hospital corps company that did excellent service in later years when inducted into the world war service. In buying supplies I used common business diligence and secured prices below those usually paid under like conditions.

By order of the governor I prepared a book of instruction for the personal care of the troops. It also illustrated the stretcher drill and prescribed conditions for enlistment in the Guard. The requirements as to weight and heighth of the regular army had been in effect in the Guard and I changed it to the West Point Academy requirements.

Perhaps the most complete and most efficient encampment and school of instruction ever held by the Nebraska National Guard under the old law, was held at Hastings, August 20th to 25th, 1900. It was a brigade encampment named Camp Lee Forby in honor of Lee Forby a member of the First Nebraska who lost his life in the Philippine campaign. The brigade composed of the First and Second reorganized Regiments, Troop "A" of Seward, Battery "A" of Wymore, and First and Second Regimental Bands. By order of the governor, Gen. Barry assumed command of the Brigade encampment and I of the medical department as brigade surgeon.

The camp grounds and assignments of the different units and camp accessories followed the most advanced military rules. It was a working school of instruction, and individual drill in manual of arms, squad drill, company drill, battalion drill, artillery and cavalry drill had their periods assigned them. The rest periods were short.

Inspection of quarters, kitchens and dining tents, kitchen sinks, and latrines was made by medical officers. The medical department instructed in the proper way to safeguard the sleeping quarters against rain by digging a shallow trench around the outside. At fatigue in the morning, flaps of tents were ordered spread back, bedding aired and be ready for medical inspection. I made the inspection each morning accompanied by a medical officer. This school of instruction was the crowning effort of General Barry's military experience and was highly successful. War with China seemed probable and the call for a Nebraska regiment was expected. Both First and Second Regiments were anxious to answer the call.

The experience of the Second Nebraska at Chickamauga Park and apparent incompetency of the medical department of the United States in caring for the sick in all places, was so deplorable that the

Commander-in-Chief was anxious that the reorganization of the medical department of the Nebraska National Guard be made as thorough and efficient as possible. I was given every opportunity and treated with courtesy. My reports were embodied in the Adjutant General's reports. The National Military Surgeons Association, of which I was a member, invited me to read a paper at the annual meeting in Boston.

In making his report to the governor of the activities at Camp Lee Forby, Gen. Barry had this to say about my department:

"I am pleased to commend to Your Excellency the splendid work in the medical department in charge of Surgeon General Barns, and in particular the first aid to the wounded. In the Hospital Corps one hundred men were trained to litter drill. The drill work was such as lifting the wounded and carrying them to the hospital and again removing them from the litter. This was all done in accordance with the manual published by Surgeon General Barns."

The work of the school of instruction closed with a brigade parade and inspection by the governor and his staff. It was a pretentious and brilliant affair. It was made more effectual and realistic by the number of officers and men who had recently been enrolled in the U. S. Volunteer service, and engaged in the Spanish war or insurrection campaign in the Philippines.

Other experiences arose that gave the brigade an example of real war. After the brigade review at Camp Lee Forby, discipline relaxed to give many men down town liberty. Perry Law, a member of

Company L, Second Regiment, recruited at Norfolk, was assaulted and beaten cruelly in a saloon down town. His First Sergeant rescued him and with great difficulty returned him to camp where his condition looked so serious that his company comrades at once went down town with the avowed purpose of taking immediate revenge on the saloon proprietor and his barkeeper. The injured private was so violent that I had to order him to the guard house and had him roped to hold him to dress his injuries. Soon a call came from town that 2,000 soldiers were mobbing the town and help was asked. Practically the entire brigade marched down town and I detailed a medical unit to accompany them and treat the injured. Captain Hartigan of D Company, Second Regiment, from Fairbury was in command of the provost guard. He threw a line around the offending saloon that had already been partly wrecked. After a turbulent night, order was restored and the state had to pay a tidy sum later for the damage that had been done to the saloon building.

The night before brigade inspection Gov. Poynter was given a banquet at the principal hotel in town to which the heads of departments were ined. Before separating, a wind, rain and hail storm, came up that almost attained the magnitude of a tornado. Half the tents in camp were blown down, men were rain soaked and suffered much from cold before morning and thus got a real taste of the hardships of camp.

The success of the encampment may be shown from the civilians' view point from reports given by the daily papers at the time. The following was clipped from the lengthy daily newspaper reports of the Hastings National Guard Encampment:

"Public attention, which was so vividly drawn to Nebraska's state soldiery during the Spanish-American war, was again brushed up by the annual state encampment of that organization at Hastings week before last, where again were enacted scenes of military life, and where again were the young men of the state infused with military ardor which comes in a practical way only from the hard work of drilling and camping. This was the first brigade encampment since 1897, and the first time that the younger men of the Nebraska National Guard had a chance to avail themselves of the benefit of association in camp with the veterans of the Philippines.

The practical work of this encampment was what did the old-timers in state military affairs good to see. Prior to the Spanish-American war the men of experience in the field were almost unknown among the state troops. At this encampment, fully 25 per cent of the national guardsmen were ex-volunteers of the Spanish-American war, and had seen something of the rough side of military life. Since this element practically made up all the officers and "non-coms," it was the dominating influence in camp.

Somehow, among the men who have been in the field, the pomp and glory of the thing doesn't find expression in elaborate dress uniforms with a superabundance of glittering tin and brass."

"This force is organized into one brigade for camp purposes, although it has no brigadier general and staff as such. At camp, Adjutant General Patrick H. Barry, in his capacity as brigadier general.

assumed command, and formed the brigade staff from that of the governor's headquarters staff, and from officers detailed from the various commands in camp.

As an instance of this consolidation of officers, Colonel C. G. Barns, surgeon general, was made chief brigade surgeon. He then organized a brigade hospital department in lieu of regimental hospitals, by calling in Captain Charles L. Mullins, chief surgeon of the First regiment, and Captain Arthur P. Ginn, chief surgeon of the Second regiment. With them went their hospital stewards, Dr. J. H. Hungate of the First, and Dr. C. W. Walden of the Second regiment.

In this way, could be more effectively carried on the work of instruction in hospital work, in which four men from each and every company in the state must be familiarized.

During every day in camp, the care of the sick, first aid to the wounded, and their care on the battle-field and in hospitals was taught to a class of 100, and drill in litter work, such as the lifting of the wounded, the carrying to hospital, and the removal from the litters, was carried out. This was done according to the new manual published for the Nebraska National Guard by Surgeon General Barns. Then on the last day, each company was presented with a hospital corps pouch, each containing four manuals, rolls of gauze and antiseptic bandages; a tourniquet, a surgeon's knife, scissors, a first aid package, wire splints, and other necessities for emergency work. This outfit was taken home by each company along with the litter it already had for practical instruction, and to have on hand for use, if necessary, and as each company is subject to instant call for the suppression of riots or invasions, it may be of use at any time."

Colonel Stotsenburg was killed in battle in the Philippines and his body returned to the United States and burial in the National Cemetery at Arlington. At Lincoln a military funeral was given at the church he attended while Commandant at the State University. His body laid in state in the state house under military escort. He was a great soldier and while some members of the First Regiment, who desired to return home after the Spanish military forces had surrendered, complained at his discipline, they recognized his worth and his reason for such discipline when the active campaign against the natives brought them into danger.

The Nebraska National Guard was built upon the foundation laid by the magnificent fighting men of territorial Nebraska. Legalized as a National Guard in 1881, ten years later they participated in the campaign that was the last clash with American Indians under tribal government. Their history is an honorable one and they have honored their state.